I0112429

A New Bretton Woods for a New World

Reflections on the Future 80 Years After the Bretton Woods Conference

Giovanni Tria and Angelo Federico Arcelli

Transatlantic Leadership Network

Giovanni Tria and Angelo Federico Arcelli, *A New Bretton Woods for a New World*

© Transatlantic Leadership Network, 2024.

ISBN: 9781737049159

Published by
Transatlantic Leadership Network
1800 M St NW #33161
Washington, D.C. 20036-5828

Distributed by
Casemate Group
www.casemategroup.com

Contents

Foreword

In this volume, Giovanni Tria and Angelo Federico Arcelli continue their review of the international monetary system, which they began with their earlier study, "Towards a Renewed Bretton Woods Agreement", which we published in 2020. They review how we got here, discuss the pros and cons of the current system, point to challenges, and offer thoughtful options for the future.

The U.S. dollar remains the global anchor currency, despite efforts to displace it. Yet the United States faces geopolitical and geoeconomic challenges that raise questions about the sustainability of current structures. U.S. debt continues to rise. Russia wants to conquer Ukraine and subjugate its neighbors. China seeks alternative global arrangements. Emerging economies demand a larger voice commensurate with their growing weight in the global economy. The countries of the eurozone often chafe under U.S. tutelage, yet have a vested in interest in stability, and seem unable to come together around more ambitious efforts at unity. While there is dissatisfaction with the current system, the alternatives could be worse.

In the spirit of prompting reflective thinking about the future of the transatlantic relationship, the Transatlantic Leadership Network is pleased to publish the second volume by our two distinguished authors in our series on the international monetary system.

Daniel S. Hamilton
President
Transatlantic Leadership Network

Introduction[1,2]

Today we may be on the verge of significant change in the global monetary system, driven by the changing nature of globalization and by the digital revolution, with all its consequences. These two forces will recast the global economic landscape.

The Bretton Woods system established in the aftermath of the Second World War afforded the United States an "exorbitant privilege" as the owner and sole issuer of the world's central currency, the U.S. dollar. Tensions generated by trade imbalances among the advanced economies finally led the United States in August 1971 to stop honoring the dollar peg to gold.

Since then, the international monetary system has evolved. The currencies of Western countries have been free to float without any fluctuation bands or any peg. Nevertheless, the U.S. dollar's central position in the international economy and the global trading system continues. It represents a key attribute of U.S. global leadership.[3]

After the anarchic period following the collapse of the Bretton Woods system, the dollar gradually regained its dominant role in the international monetary system. It has strengthened its position since the turn of the new century.

The role of the U.S. dollar (and somehow, in recent years, that of the euro) gives the United States and its allies powerful leverage to influence competing powers and affords the West a position of indisputable leadership beyond military and geopolitical factors. But China's rise and its determination to compete for global leadership could also include efforts to dominate international trade and payment settlements. Growing tensions among major powers and the advent of new digital tools, including payment instruments and crypto assets, have created a challenging environment for central banks.

For a time, pegging the renminbi to the dollar was useful for China's industrialization, which was driven by exports. On one hand, more recently China started to push for a reshape of the international monetary system, which could reduce the role of the U.S. dollar. The United States and its main allies, on the other hand, want to protect the role of the U.S. dollar, to the point of risking a "decoupling" in the international monetary system. Meanwhile, the EU is struggling to find a stable equilibrium amid economic and geopolitical upheavals resulting from Russia's invasion of Ukraine.

But today's currencies, including the dollar, seem to have lost "intrinsic" value because they are not pegged at a given fixed exchange rate to any commodity, such as gold. Nonetheless, in addition to serving as a unit of account and medium of exchange, a currency can retain its full function as a store of value, but solely because everyone accepts it as a means of payment. This acceptance assumes that the currency does not "lose value" per se - as if it were a substitute for gold - and this is possible if there is a well-founded belief that it does not depreciate relative to other currencies and their relative purchasing power. If there is inflation, what matters is that a currency's purchasing power does not decline more than other currencies or means of exchange. These conditions still give the dollar the role of anchor international currency. But the stability of the dollar's purchasing power is enabled by a de facto exchange rate peg guaranteed by growing dollar reserves, and dollar-denominated securities, which represent safe assets par excellence.

What does it mean to say that U.S. dollars are safe assets? It means precisely that the sale of these safe assets, currency and securities, in exchange for other currencies or real assets, will not predictably result in losses (beyond worldwide inflation that does not change the relative value of currencies). This is possible if the demand for dollars and dollar securities remains such that the supply of dollars is balanced. This on the one hand requires that U.S.

monetary policy not flood the world with excess dollars and on the other hand that a U.S. positive capital account balance compensates for a current account deficit, that is, a demand for dollars that avoids their depreciation.

At the same time, to keep pace with the growth of international trade, the U.S. Federal Reserve, the country's central bank, has to offer dollars, thus increasing U.S. debt. If U.S. GDP is bound to shrink as a share of global GDP, to keep the supply of dollars stable relative to global GDP the United States would have to continually increase its debt as a percentage of its GDP. This is Triffin's critique in a new context: in the long run, growing U.S. debt is unsustainable. To summarize: maintaining the dollar's role as the world's anchor currency requires both demand for dollars and the ability to offer them sustainably.

What has changed from Bretton Woods is that the U.S. dollar today is not convertible into gold, but, as the system still has the dollar as the global currency, that implies that it maintains its central role in the foreign exchange market, and this means that U.S. monetary policy must be pandered to by the rest of the world. In other words, in the absence of gold, the confidence reflected in the stability of the U.S. dollar value in the market determines the stability of the system based on the dollar as the global currency.

The conclusion would eventually be that the value of the dollar is based only on trust. Also the value of other alternatives, such as BitCoins is based only on trust, albeit those are not really currencies. They have no stability of value at all, since there is no central bank behind them. Instead, they are speculative "commodities," with floating values. BitCoins and other cryptocurrencies are normally exchanged against the U.S. dollar to recognize their market value, which implies a dependency on the international currency system to allow for their usage (purchase and selling). As a means of payment, they can be exchanged for a stable currency or for purchases of real goods, but, given their volatility, they are hardly a store of value. This is because the value of BitCoins is based only on the confidence they can gather. They have no legal tender base, as no authority regulates them. Thus, they remain speculative tools that are used precisely in the expectation of potential positive change in their value, so not at all useful for operators who seek stability.

The situation is different when it comes to stable coins, which share with BitCoins the absence of a national or supranational authority to regulate their issuance but are based on an underlying basket of national currencies and, therefore, represent the real challenge to currencies issued by central banks and can contend with their role as a means of payment and in theory also as store of value, because they can share in the stability of the underlying basket of currencies. The weakness of cryptocur rencies is that they cannot compete with currencie s issued by central banks, which are the ones actually setting the rules of the monetary system.. This is where central bank digital currencies (CBDCs) come in.

What are the prospects? The current system's weakness is the dangerous yet necessary expansion of U.S. debt. We do not know when this weakness may manifest itself. A multipolar solution may be the gradual erosion of the need to maintain the dollar as the global currency to which other currencies are pegged. The reasons for erosion have been discussed, but the process could be accelerated by geopolitical issues, such as decoupling, the weaponization of interdependence or exploitation of "exorbitant privilege." However, an effective multipolar situation requires that China remove institutional and political obstacles to renminbi convertibility and greater Chinese capital mobility, so that it could play a balancing role in issuing sufficient safe assets alongside U.S. assets.

This is not a short-to-medium-term prospect because it also implies a Chinese willingness to move toward internationalization of the renminbi, which would go beyond increasing its role as a means of payment in bilateral trade. This appears to be the needed condition for moving toward the idea of a "bancor," the global currency imagined by Keynes, whose underlying anchor should be an enlarged basket of strong currencies. It would be the transformation into currency of a kind of Special Drawing Right (SDR) which, however, in addition to implying an international issuing institution, should always be based on a changed role of the national reference currencies and thus a new role for the renminbi. This idea implies the need to imagine a process of rapprochement to a global "anchor" currency like the negotiating path that led to the euro, and it is no coincidence that the rapprochement process consisted at the beginning of a mutual peg agreement between national European currencies.

What practical possibility exists for moving toward one or the other solution? It is necessary to look at the political interests of countries, particularly those whose other attributes—technology, military power, institutional soundness—are as dominant as their currencies. Changing the current situation does not suit the United States. To some extent it does not suit Europe either, because even though Europe seeks autonomy, it partially and reflexibly shares the "exorbitant privilege" of the current system. Europe would probably have less political and economic space in a more multipolar world.

The rest of the world does not necessarily share the same interests as the West, however, and therefore the balance of power that will come to be determined for demographic and economic reasons, and to some extent technological and military balances, require an adjustment toward a system where regulation is more shared. Hence, the interest, then, of the Western world seems to be to prevent unwelcome changes, and thus to "negotiate" a more shared governance of the international monetary system and international trade—a new Bretton Woods agreement.

For the West and the United States, it is a matter of trading short-term advantages for a less unstable or dangerous prospect. It is a matter of investing today to maintain centrality or at least not to lose a decisive role in the future.

The digital revolution is silently influencing all agendas. The shift in the available set of payment tools that it represents is putting such pressure on central banks worldwide that the idea of developing CBDCs is gaining traction. The development of CBDCs is a defensive move aimed at maintaining full control of monetary policy. Suppose they become reality in Western countries, which seems likely. In that case, this could lead to the need for a new deal and, possibly, a renewed IMF treaty, if not even a new stability guardian, empowered to intervene in a different monetary landscape.

Will it be something planned (as evidenced by the growing introduction of CBDCs on different platforms) or will it result from the growing challenge to traditional monetary tools currently represented by cryptocurrencies, digital currencies, and all the other monetary tools that are starting to be widely used, including in Western countries?

The recent international landscape is marked by great uncertainty. We are witnessing a period of change, marked by emerging global geopolitical competition and growing stress on a weaponized monetary system,[4] which have generated doubts about the safety of trade and supply chains and the role of money.[5] The European project is also at stake, at least until a clear path to a political union or a credible alternative is defined.[6]

Until recently it was widely believed that economic progress would lead to liberal democratic values spreading worldwide. Now there is growing awareness that a reasonable level and diffusion of economic well-being does not necessarily require liberal democracy. The shocking question that emerges, therefore, is whether the link between Western liberal democracy and market economy is the only possible marriage, or whether or it will remain a choice or a privilege for only part of humankind.

The Chinese case, then, is relevant for a long-term view of such issues as development, trade and democracy. Over the past thirty years, the enormous growth of the Chinese economy - driven by the entry into the World Trade Organization (WTO) and the creation of significant trade ties with Western economies and the United States in particular—was not accompanied by the development of a Western-style economic or political system. Rather,

China remains a relatively centralized system and a significantly successful example of economic development that is far from EU and U.S. models.

Our analysis, drawing on aprevious work,[7] will start by recalling, in the first two chapters, the historical background that led to the Bretton Woods agreements and the continuous quest for stability and efficiency in the exchange rate system and international trade. In the following three chapters, some reflections are presented both on the weaknesses of the system agreed at Bretton Woods, that led to its collapse in August 1971, and on the reasons which led, de facto, again to a U.S. dollar-centered international monetary system, even after the creation of the single European currency and the China's accession to the WTO. We will also describe in these chapters how even this de facto system, by some referred to as the Second Bretton Woods, preserves much of the characteristics and, consequently, of the weaknesses of the system established in 1944, while in a different global macroeconomic and political context. Moreover, many factors which allowed it to survive until now are expected to weaken, even due to current de-globalization and protectionism trends which represent growing factors of uncertainty. In the last three chapters we will analyze more how the conditions which have enabled the dollar to be kept as a linchpin of the international monetary system over the past few decades are weakening, endangering its sustainability, beyond its contested desirability, also in the face of the challenges posed by the spread of new digital currencies and means of payment. Finally, we propose some ideas about the desirability, if not the necessity, of a shared path for the reform of the international monetary system, to govern the future evolution also to mitigate the uncertainties, and of the international institutions, both to regain authority and legitimacy, and to ensure a sustainable new agreement.

1

Behind the Quest for an International Monetary Balancing Mechanism[8]

Throughout history, international orders have been constructed, contested, upended and dismantled. The current international financial order, which has led the world to a relatively stable system since the end of World War II, was defined at a conference held in 1944 at the Mount Washington Hotel in Bretton Woods, New Hampshire.[9] The conference resulted in the creation of a mechanism to govern monetary, commercial and financial relations among members, aiming to be a worldwide order.

The outcome of the conference was the establishment of a set of international institutions tasked with ensuring the stability and function of the system, namely the International Monetary Fund (IMF), guardian of monetary stability and trade, and the World Bank, primarily focused on development. Both institutions were created in 1945. In the following years the General Agreement on Tariffs and Trade (GATT) gradually became the main forum for trade disputes, and in 1995 it became the World Trade Organization (WTO).

Although in the immediate aftermath of World War II the international system had been strengthened by the creation of institutions and fora in charge of ensuring stability and dialogue, this was not the case in the previous period. The system historically in place, the Gold Standard (later the Gold Exchange Standard)[10] did not need any permanent institution as it was originally a mere convertibility right of tender notes (bank notes) in a defined amount of gold, or, in a defined proportion, silver; or (for the Gold Exchange Standard) also in defined convertible tender notes of different currencies, in turn accepted by their issuing central bank as convertible in gold or silver.

The Gold Standard system system was meant to adjust naturally to changes in the relative market values of the two metals. Indeed, the mint parity could differ from the market relative price of the two metals. When it did, one or the other metal would go out of circulation. For example, if the price of gold in terms of silver increased, no one would want to turn gold into gold dollar coins at the mint. More dollars would be obtained by instead using the gold to buy silver in the market, and then having the silver coined into dollars. As a result, gold coins would tend to go out of monetary circulation when its relative market price rose above the mint relative price[11].

This system operated "naturally" and did not require an institution to manage the circulation of the metals. In theory, the price stability achieved by the Gold Standard (then Gold Exchange Standard, as for the Bretton Woods mechanism) pegged system could be considered beneficial for trade and the global economy. Nevertheless, what the world had already experienced in late 19th century was the constraint that the availability of gold reserves had on money supply, which meant, essentially, a very limited capability for states to have an active monetary policy (which was needed and possible during wartime only, as the convertibility was suspended) with all its consequences.[12]

The Gold Standard also tended to run the risk of exporting financial crises, a phenomenon nowadays known as contagion. Therefore, given that countries adhering to gold convertibility were tightly linked to each other by the fixed exchange rates of their gold parities and, because of the absence of serious impediments to the flow of goods and capital, the transmission of shocks was facilitated between countries, including financial crises.[13]

There is also some empirical evidence that shows that the Gold Standard had positive effects on price stability. In Britain and the United States, real per capita income was less variable between 1870 and 1913 than it was thereafter. Although this long, stable period was recorded in the then wealthiest countries, for the rest of the world the Gold Standard did not lead to the same stability. In the 19th and early 20th centuries, the short-run fluctuations in gold prices were partly a result of changes in the global stock of gold, which more than tripled between the 1850s and 1900s.[14]

As the Gold Standard is a monetary system where a country fixes the price of its currency to gold, in this type of system, no single country occupies a privileged position, in contrast to the Bretton Woods system. As an international system, its primary function was to fix exchange rates, or to be precise, narrow the band of fluctuation down to the so called "gold points", the rate at which it became profitable to import or export gold.

Although the Gold Standard dates back to 1821—when the British Parliament resumed its practice of exchanging currency notes for gold on demand at a fixed rate—it was only after 1871 that countries gradually abandoned silver in favour of the monometallic Gold Standard. In 1868, only Britain, and several of its economic dependencies, were on the Gold Standard.[15]

World events, however, complicated the functioning of the bimetallic system. For example, large gold discoveries increased the supply of gold, decreasing its price and, therefore, increasing the relative price of silver. This would, on the other hand, put pressure on the fixed exchange rate system. Moreover, silver coins would eventually be removed from circulation.

Some countries responded to these events by producing subsidiary silver coins. These were small silver coins whose metallic value was less than the coin's face value, essentially debasing the coins. Those coins were less likely to be withdrawn from the market and, therefore, were available to support commerce. This enabled states to debase their currencies relative to the other members, meaning that they could include fewer precious metals in their currency and exchange it for the currency of their fellow members, resulting in a profit for them.

The first such instance of currency debasement occurred almost instantly after the Latin Monetary Union was formed.[16] In an attempt to establish the bimetallic system on an international scale, France, Belgium, Italy, the Papal States and Switzerland formed the Latin Monetary Union (LMU) in 1865.

These four founding states agreed to mint their coins according to the French standard, which was introduced in 1803 by Napoleon Bonaparte, and they guaranteed the acceptability of each member's coins in all member states. The standard dictated that while each nation would be allowed to mint its own currency, this currency had to follow a specific set of guidelines. Because it was a bimetallic system, the coins issued had to be silver or gold. These coins could then be exchanged at a rate of 15.5 silver coins to one gold coin. These specifications were agreed to enhance trade and the flow of goods between the member states.

The Latin Monetary Union[17] lasted (theoretically) until 1927.[18] It included all the main Latin-speaking language countries (a group led by France[19]), which agreed to share a bimetallic system where both silver and gold coins could circulate.[20] In addition, free coinage meant that anyone could bring metal to the mint to be coined into gold or silver money.[21]

The interwar period, including the long depression that resulted after the 1929 crisis, had already proven that a multilateral scheme based on the Gold Exchange Standard was not optimal, and was only possible given that gold reserves were primarily held in few states' central banks, and, ultimately, unfit to respond to a global financial crisis. During World War I, the Gold Exchange Standard mechanism was suspended. After the war ended, national and international debt became an international issue again as government finances deteriorated to support the management of the war aftermath and the rebuilding of industries.

Clearly the need to suspend the mechanism during a period of war demonstrated a key weakness, and eventual inadequacy to manage the global economy through both good and bad times. It became increasingly apparent that the world needed something more flexible to ensure both monetary stability and the growing international trade.[22]

The heavy burden of payment imposed on Germany after the peace treaty led to a monetary crisis around 1920-23 and to even more dire consequences.[23] As a matter of fact, it was only by 1928 that the Gold Exchange Standard mechanism had been re-established internationally. Its resumption of normal activities lasted for a short time, as the subsequent 1929 crisis and the Great Depression led to the progressive abandoning of the system over the 1930s.[24] World War II, with the return to the same situation of World War I for currencies, seemed to represent the tombstone for an era.

While World War II was still blazing, the United States and Great Britain set about to remake the Wilsonian order, preserving its basic principles while innovating the institutional design. As the only great power to have avoided the destruction of World War II, the United States quickly became the operator of this new order.[25]

As the Bretton Woods agreements were a landmark in defining the new architecture of the international monetary system, we should not forget how much the world had changed with respect to the schemes used before and their downfall.[26]

At the end of World War II, the United States was alone accounted for around 50% of the world's GDP, and, although the percentage was quickly shrinking in the following years, this facilitated the definition of a scheme which mirrored the preferred option. of U.S. negotiator Harry Dexter White, prevailed over Keynes' idea for the multilateral currency, the "bancor," which never saw the light of day.[27]

Table 1

World GDP in 1950 (PPP)[28]

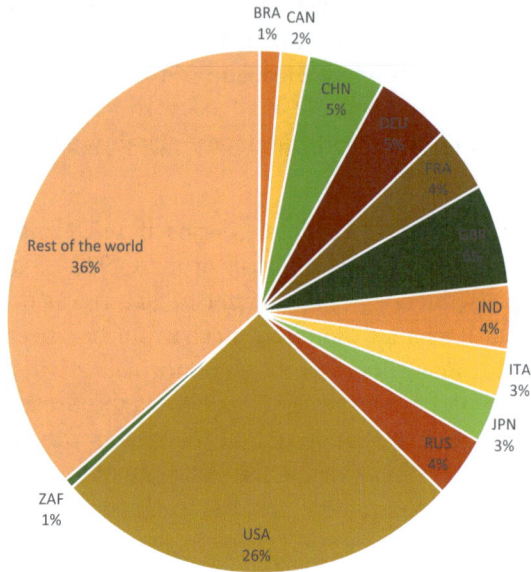

The return of the European powers to pre-war GDP levels, and their subsequent relevant growth in the 1960s, gradually reduced the relative weight of the United States in world GDP. This global power shift not only reduced American hegemony (the U.S. share of global GDP diminished as a percentage of the total) but created the conditions for several changes of the original scheme over time, notably the abandoning of gold convertibility in 1971.

Amidst these dynamics, all commentators recognize that new orders have often followed dark epochs and often institutions need to be reshaped to fit together and become the cornerstone for future construction.[29] After World War II, to avoid the turbulence of the Great Depression period, it was decided that exchange rates had to be fixed to the dollar, which in turn was tied to gold. Members of the IMF contributed their currencies and gold to form a pool of financial resources that the IMF could lend to countries in need.[30]

Table 2

World GDP in 1971 (PPP)[31]

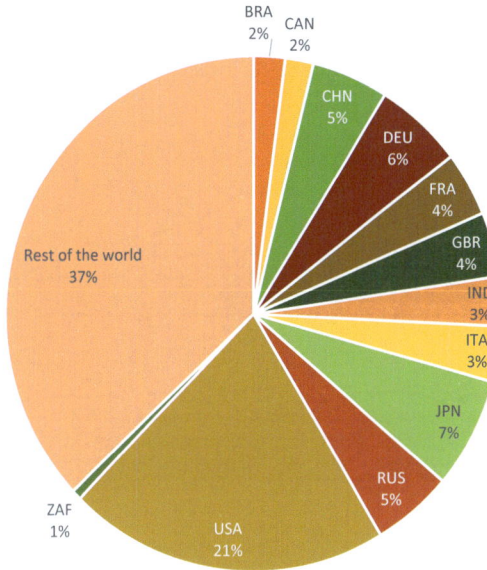

The drawback of this system was that there was an inherent asymmetry that eventually led to policy disputes. Moreover, the United States, which occupied a special position within the system, experienced large current account deficits and needed to depreciate its currency. These and other drawbacks led to the breakup of the Bretton Woods system in 1971.

With the end of the Bretton Woods system on August 13th, 1971, when the United States decided to end the era of the Gold Exchange Standard, Western European countries were forced to give up the convertibility of their currencies, and exchange rates started to float. In the wake of such change, financial and monetary stability suddenly seemed to be at stake.

Table 3

Official Gold Reserves of Central Banks[32]

Volume of GOLD in millions of fine troy ounces

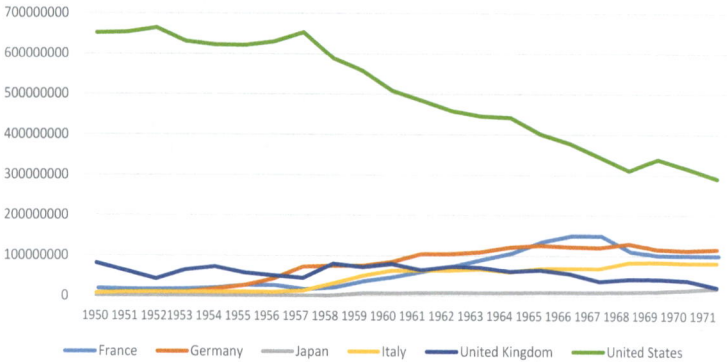

As a result, Europe reacted with the Werner plan in 1973. Europe was at a new dawn, trying to find a new equilibrium.[33] The birth of the European Monetary System (EMS) scheme focused on the German Deutsche Mark at its core seemed to create such new stability. It developed a new figurative currency, the European Currency Unit (ECU). It was not the first time in history that Europe aimed to a coordinated scheme for the currencies used in the continent. The first one occurred in 1865 and was known as the Latin Union. But the agreement of 1865 was essentially a scheme based on the common usage of the Gold Standard mechanism.

2

Towards a Single Currency in Europe

After the end of the U.S. dollar-centred Bretton Woods era in 1971, it took two years for the Europeans to cope with their need for a stable system to anchor their currencies. The Werner plan in 1973 seemed a feasible solution, in the wake of oil crisis which accelerated the process and forced Western European states to resolve their differences. It led to the establishment of the European Monetary System (EMS) in 1979, which, despite several realignments among strong and weak currencies, seemed to be reasonably stable. In fact, by removing any exchange rate risk and affirming a country's commitment to sound fiscal and monetary policies, the system should have reduced the cost of international borrowing for all member countries.

This was a commitment mechanism; countries could not pursue time-inconsistent fiscal and monetary policies such as printing money to collect seigniorage or playing with public debt, as the market would have punished them by putting pressure on central bank reserves and imposing a rebalancing of parities. The combination of long-run price stability, a commitment to time-consistent fiscal and monetary policies and lower interest payments on foreign debt made, in theory, the EMS quite attractive.

When the treaty of Maastricht was signed in January 1992, the decision to create limits and constraints to public spending, deficits and debts seemed to be the right way for moving towards a new

Table 4

Conversion Rates to the Euro[34]

Adoption	Country	Currency	Fixed conversion rates
1999	Belgium	Belgian francs	40.3399
	Germany	Deutsche Mark	1.95583
	Spain	Spanish pesetas	166.386
	France	French francs	6.55957
	Ireland	Irish pound	0.787564
	Italy	Italian lire	1936.27
	Luxembourg	Luxembourg francs	40.3399
	The Netherlands	Dutch guilders	2.20371
	Austria	Austrian schillings	13.7603
	Portugal	Portuguese escudos	200.482
	Finland	Finnish markkas	5.94573
2001	Greece	Greek drachmas	340.75
2007	Slovenia	Slovenian tolars	239.64
2008	Cyprus	Cypriot pound	0.585274
	Malta	Maltese lira	0.4293
2009	Slovakia	Slovak koruna	30.126
2011	Estonia	Estonian kroon	15.6466
2014	Latvia	Latvian lats	0.702804
2015	Lithuania	Lithuanian litas	3.4528
2023	Croatia	Croatian kruna	7.5345

strong currency, one with the potential of challenging the exorbitant privilege of the only true reserve currency, the U.S. dollar. The Black Wednesday crisis of September 1992 was a major hit for this ambitious project, but it was a temporary setback.[35]

From the Delors Plan to the Euro

Notwithstanding such temporary setbacks, the path outlined by the Delors plan continued, and, in April 1998, all major EU member states took a giant leap towards closer monetary integration. They agreed on the introduction of a new single currency, the euro, to be circulated as paper bills as of January 1, 2002. Initially the new euro seemed strong. Markets priced it above the U.S. dollar, at least initially, when it was traded at around 0.85 for the dollar.[36] It was politics, and the vision for a new Europe, that had prevailed over economics and the voices of those who suggested that the new monetary union was not an optimal currency area, as it was not only postponing significant steps towards closer fiscal integration, but it was at the same time accepting economically weaker members that were not yet able to live within the constraints of a common currency. However, at the time critical voices were drowned out by a consensus that saw Europe inevitably moving closer. The agreement on the common currency seemed to be enough to sustain the drive towards an even closer union.[37]

But the 1998 agreements were the result of the deal between German Chancellor Helmut Kohl and French President François Mitterrand and the political view born in the early 1990s (still supported by Chirac after 1995) when Germany was reunified. A reunited Germany regained its full national sovereignty and triggered some deep-seated anxieties among its neighbours, most notably France. France wanted a larger euro area to not be "alone" in a potentially unequal partnership with Germany. To achieve this objective, Italy and others, despite their shaky public finances, could participate from the very beginning to the project. The political decision of both German and French leaderships to refuse a "two speed" Europe and push for a single Europe, single market, single currency approach, coupled with a belief that the EU would inevitably continue to move towards closer political integration, allowed the euro to materialize as it was conceived.

Despite some initial difficulties, such as the narrow French referendum in 1994, the consensus among EU members on the perspective of a European Union, as a political body in the long run, remained strong.[38] Against this background, the pledge to keep public deficits within a narrow range of GDP (3%) under the European Stability Pact, and the commitment for a long-term target of public debt to GDP ratios at or below 60%, seemed enough to provide the necessary underpinnings for a progressive convergence of European economies.[39]

Unfortunately, the attempt in 2003 to reshape EU governing rules failed. When ten new member states joined the EU in 2004, and another two joined in 2007, the burdensome decisional architecture showed its limits, with too many people sitting at the same table trying to make decisions under the constant threat of multiple cross-vetoes, only able to make difficult compromises based on very low common denominators. While Europe as a political project stalled, so did the convergence of different economies. Only some of them had a single currency.

Table 5

Development of Spreads in Interest Rates on
Sovereign Bonds (as Compared to German Bonds)[40]

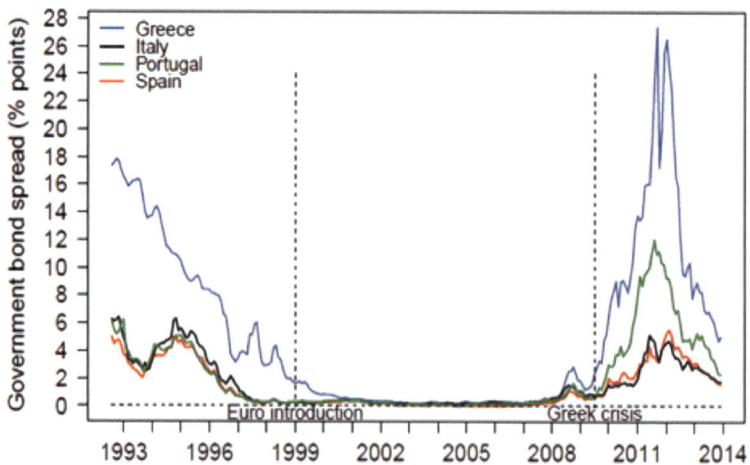

Source: WEF

The euro was born with a flawed architecture.[41] It was, and, still, remains, the common currency for economies that exhibit strong substantive differences in fiscal as well as in macroeconomic performance. Furthermore, the euro was born with no single treasury behind it. Instead, it relies on a central bank that has a very narrow mandate of price stability.[42] The treaty confines the European Central Bank (ECB) to the role of ensuring the stability of the system rather than an instrument of economic support through monetary policy (like the U.S. Federal Reserve).[43]

The decisions of 1998 left fiscal policies in Europe in the hands of national governments. Brussels had limited say, or at least, no effective means to enforce rules. Despite these flaws, for a decade, markets implicitly accepted the convergence theory. Sovereign bond spreads between eurozone countries were, in fact, quite limited for a decade (1998-2008).

The burden of past public debt and inefficiencies could have been a major impediment to launching the euro, but financial markets simply assumed that European economic growth would facilitate convergence and the debt burden would prove to be manageable even in higher debt economies. In short, the euro was a currency launched without an adequate institutional foundation, or, as events a decade later proved, the political commitment to sustain it.

The Lehman Crisis and the Response in Europe in the Following Decade

The Lehman crisis in September 2008 was the spark for a debt crisis that rapidly involved banks, non-financial corporations, households and, last, but not least, national governments. Initially, it was primarily the banking sector's stability that was at stake, worldwide and in Europe.[44]

Governments reacted by supporting the banking system with guarantees, capital and debt. To avoid a deep recession, many countries supported collapsing demand by expanding public spending.

Both actions stretched public finances and increased sovereign deficits and debts. Rather than act in concert, each eurozone member supported its "own" banks.[45]

This choice was perceived by markets as the end of European convergence: risk was shifting from commercial (banks) to sovereigns (states), but in an uneven manner: each was on its own.

Economic fundamentals in each member country came under much more scrutiny. Markets quickly began to re-price national risk. As a result, borrowing costs for the highly indebted eurozone (the so-called "PIIGS"—Portugal, Ireland, Italy, Greece and Spain) countries spiked. Even though the default of a sovereign eurozone borrower was now no longer unthinkable; it was still a reasonably remote case. But investors started to factor in the danger of incurring real losses.

The sovereign debt crisis in Europe was triggered by the Greek case. In 2009 the Greek government had to admit that for years it had in essence cooked the books, to meet the stringent Maastricht criteria and gain full membership in the monetary union. The government in Athens finally conceded that its real deficit was much higher at over 13%, versus a previous estimate of around 4%. The awareness of the high level of interconnection among European economies and the fact that the main German and French banks were overexposed forced EU governments to rescue weaker countries as the situation deteriorated. In Greece, as well as in Portugal and Ireland, this was the start of the age of bailouts.[46]

But Ireland, a eurozone member, was broadly supported and attracted the intervention of the United Kingdom (which is not a eurozone member). The government in London saw its own national interests at stake. Portugal was supported by EU members and institutions and started a bold program of reforms and tax increases. However, it did not prove to be enough to shield the country from contagion. Indeed, Portugal was the first victim of a different perception of sovereign risk by markets.[47]

The case of Greece was different from the very beginning, as Greek banks were largely foreign owned (in particular, by French and German groups) and Greece was already overleveraged in terms of public debt because of its decision to join the eurozone.[48] In Greece the banks, the real economy and public finances were all extremely vulnerable, even in good times. To limit potential losses to its creditors, the "price" for the bailouts (over time funded by public money—coming from the European troika, a.k.a. the IMF, European Commission, and ECB—and commercial banks through "voluntary" debt forgiveness) was the introduction of austerity: deep public spending cuts, savings and higher taxes.[49]

In other words, the concern for the stronger European economies was first and foremost to control the situation. This implied that creditors would only commit to just enough solidarity to keep countries afloat, and only in exchange for serious commitments to significant debt/deficit reduction measures and spending controls. Such measures would have been far more effective in a different, more benign macroeconomic environment before the crisis. And while they remain essential if one wishes to think of a long-term converging Europe, they are inevitably contractionary if imposed in an economic recession, thus making it very difficult for Greece and Europe to recover and grow.[50]

Indeed, those measures generally failed (at least in a first phase) to bring down yields for sovereign bonds substantially as spreads amongst "strong" and "weak" states remained significant and the associated fall in economic activity caused a vicious circle. Austerity deepened the recession. The recession worsened the fiscal situation of many countries with deficits coming down too slowly and the debt to GDP ratio increasing.[51]

This context seems now superseded by the current market trends since the start of the 2020 Covid-19 crisis, but it must be noted that current measures are apparently "temporary" and not linked to a consensus on a long-term political plan (eventually another economic plan centred on a "recovery fund," is set to be launched by 2021).

Recognizing that the Growth and Stability Pact had failed, 25 of 27 EU countries, including all eurozone countries, agreed to a new "fiscal compact" in March 2012 that would force those countries with a debt-to-GDP ratio above 60% to arrive at a structural deficit at a maximum of 0.5% and to bring the debt-to-GDP ratio back to 60% within 20 years. This target remains very ambitious and can only be met if the eurozone economies start to grow again and inflation in the eurozone can be brought back to levels closer to the target of the ECB of a rate below, but close to 2%.

In 2014, the approval of the bank recovery and resolution directive (or "BRRD", which came into force on January 1st, 2016) and the definition of a path to a "banking union" apparently paved the way for a strengthening of the banking sector, de-linking it from sovereign risks.

In the following years the possible step forward in the Banking Union project was supposed to be the extension of the role of the European Stability Mechanism (ESM) to be a partial backstop for systemic banks, according to a revision of the original treaty agreed in 2019 and which needed the positive vote of all EU parliaments to become effective[52]. But in August 2024 such new treaty has not yet been approved by all EU members.

3

The Role of the Dollar and the Quest for a New Bretton Woods

In 1944, at the Mount Washington Hotel in Bretton Woods, New Hampshire in the United States, a conference was held on how to reconstruct a new world economic order from the ruins of World War II. The leading theoretical debate was between John Maynard Keynes, representing Great Britain, and Harry Dexter White, representing the United States. White prevailed due to enhanced U.S. economic and political power.

The outcome was an international monetary system pegged to the U.S. dollar, which was convertible to gold. As a result, the dollar became the principal international reserve currency. The defeated thesis envisaged the establishment of an international currency, the "bancor."

However, in the following two decades, the system established at the Bretton Woods conference proved increasingly incapable of coping with economic and commercial imbalances among its member states. At the beginning of the 1960s the system started to be theoretically challenged by non-Keynesian economists.

The 1960s Debate on the Unsustainability of the Bretton Woods Monetary System

In 1965, Jacques Rueff,[53] French President Charles de Gaulle's economic adviser, criticized the Bretton Woods international monetary system with the famous allegory of the tailor: *"If I had an agreement with my tailor that whatever money I pay him he returns to me the very same day as a loan, I would have no objection at all to ordering more suits from him."* These were the words Jacques Rueff used to attack the Gold Exchange Standard, the system established with the 1944 Bretton Woods agreements, which had the dollar as its principal reserve currency thanks to its convertibility to gold.

Rueff's argument was that this system hindered commercial disequilibrium adjustments because the country supplying the currency convertible into gold, which is the United States, could finance its trade deficits without limits. Differing from the Gold Standard, which Rueff supported, the Gold Exchange Standard allowed the central banks of countries with a current account surplus to increase money supply based on reserves held in gold, dollar and dollar-denominated assets.

Therefore, because countries with a current account surplus that purchased dollar-denominated assets maintained, as a matter of fact, their own reserves in the U.S. central bank as dollars, the outflow of dollars from the issuing state caused by its trade deficit, did not actually determine an outflow of gold nor a decreased capacity of domestic expenditure. In other words, at the end of the 1950s and the beginning of the 1960s, this system enabled European countries and Japan to reindustrialize themselves by providing "clothes" to the United States, which was able to purchase in great amounts thanks to the credits that these country's tailors granted them.

Table 6

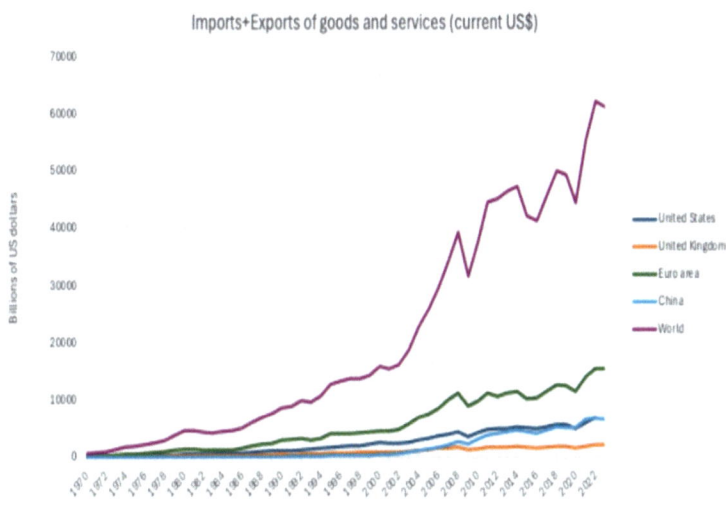

Imports+Exports of goods and services (current US$)

Table 7[54]

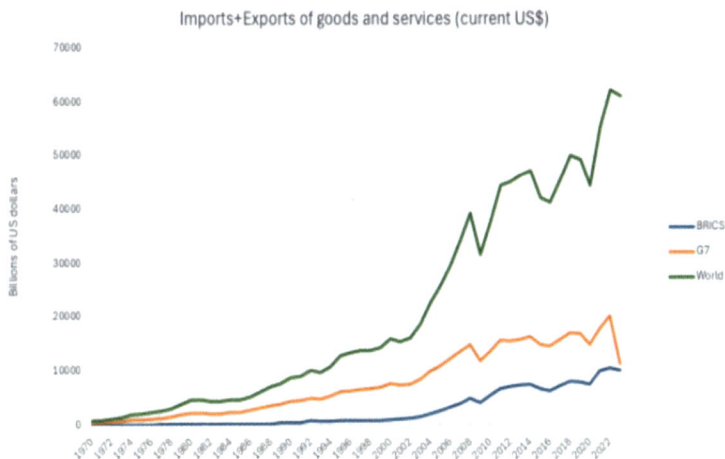

Imports+Exports of goods and services (current US$)

Rueff's analysis on the unsustainability of a system that enabled the United States to maintain permanent current account deficits was consistent with the 1960 analysis of Robert Triffin, whose critique of the Bretton Woods system would be known as the "dilemma." The Triffin dilemma is the conflict of economic interests that arises between short-term domestic and long-term international objectives for countries whose currencies serve as global reserve currencies.[55] Triffin's analysis was aligned with Rueff's analysis in that they observed that the dollars collected by the countries in surplus were used to purchase U.S. debt to hold as a reserve asset alongside gold, and, as a result, there was no mechanism to re-absorb imbalances.

The conclusion of the two economists was that, inevitably, the amount of dollars retained by the member countries would increase compared to gold, undermining the confidence in the dollar's effective convertibility. This meant declaring that the goal of the Bretton Woods conference would not be achieved, namely that of returning to a system of fixed exchange rates, while avoiding that the scarcity of gold would block, as in the Gold Standard, the supply of money requested by economic growth.[56]

Rueff and Triffin shared their diagnosis on the flaws of the Bretton Woods system but diverged on the therapy. While Rueff hoped for a return to a Gold Standard, Triffin aspired to an international monetary system based on the Keynesian "bancor," in other words, on the institution of a global currency.

From the End of the First Bretton Woods to the Second Bretton Woods

However, under the pressure of the "tailors" especially the French, who did not want to lend their revenues from the sale of their clothes to the American customer anymore, in August 1971 the U.S. announced that it would had suspended the convertibility of the dollar into gold, causing the end of the exchange system based on the Gold Exchange Standard established at the Bretton

Woods conference[57] under the pressure of the "tailors" especially the French, who did not want to lend their revenues from the sale of their clothes to the American customer anymore.

As a result, they tried to redeem their credits by asking to convert their dollar reserves into gold. From that point on, a true international monetary system—understood as several shared rules that define exchange rates between countries—has not been re-established.

Over time, there has been the establishment of a type of "anarchic" non-system, where some countries make their exchange rates fluctuate, while others peg their currencies to another foreign currency, often the dollar.

One of the notable consequences of the end of the system in place since 1944 was to leave the Europeans in need of a replacement to ensure stability to their currencies. However, this event did not compromise the role of the dollar as an international currency with its triple function as a store of value, unit of account and medium of exchange. Despite an international monetary system largely turned anarchic, that is, not guided by clear rules, the dollar maintains and reinforces a dominant role, giving the United States a so-called "exorbitant privilege." This role has never been questioned by other emerging powers, especially the more economically integrated Asian emerging countries, nor by the creation of the euro.[58]

The European countries—particularly Germany, as well as Japan and the oil producing countries have continued to strengthen their "tailoring" and the United States, as a result, has continued to buy many clothes with debt. The system has in part continued until today, with China progressively affirming itself, for the past decade, as the principal "tailor," replacing Europe and Japan. Therefore, particularly after the accession of China to the WTO in 2001, there have been talks about a "renewed" or "Second" Bretton Woods, with some of the main Asian currencies, particularly the Chinese renminbi, in addition to Latin America's currencies, pegged to the dollar alongside with controls on international capital flows between these countries and the United States.[59]

The story of this Second Bretton Woods, and the global imbalances associated with it, is instructive. The rapid Chinese economic growth coincided with its accelerated integration in the global economy. Its double-digit growth in trade with foreign countries, compared with overall growth in global trade (see table 6), generated increased and persistent trade and current account surpluses. In the three years preceding the 2008 financial crisis, the Chinese current account surplus was on average 9% of its GDP.

Until 2005, by maintaining a fixed exchange rate with the dollar and controls on financial capital outflows, China had avoided adjusting its trade imbalances for many years by accumulating official foreign reserves, which in 2011 accounted for 25% of registered central banks' global foreign reserves. China's purchase of public debt and other financial assets issued from countries with trade deficits, particularly the United States, enabled these countries to maintain high internal liquidity, therefore allowing them to sustain their internal consumption and investment demand. In addition, these purchases allowed China to control its domestic liquidity and, as a result, to control its inflation pressures.

In summary, the two sides of the Pacific neutralized the classic monetary adjustment mechanism of fixed exchange rates imbalances, namely the adjustment of real exchange rates through shifting domestic prices. The American expansionary monetary policy, which at the turn of the 20th century had fuelled the new economy and real estate market speculative bubbles, and which financed excess domestic demand, has been the other side of the coin to the Chinese central bank's policy of exchange control and trade surplus management.

Once again, the story of the Second Bretton Woods is not far from the story of Rueff's "tailor." However, even this Second Bretton Woods could not survive the 2008 financial crisis. Already in 2005, under U.S. pressure, China abandoned pegging its exchange rate to the dollar and the renminbi appreciated by about 18% in just three years (2005-2008).

The Great Financial Crisis and the Renewed Critique of the Dollar's Role

During the 2008 financial crisis, China restored its policy of pegging its currency to the dollar, at least for a few years before ultimately abandoning it again. The idea in China is that the dollar standard was no longer able to assure monetary stability in the relations between America and Asia.

Table 8

World GDP in 2008 (PPP)[60]

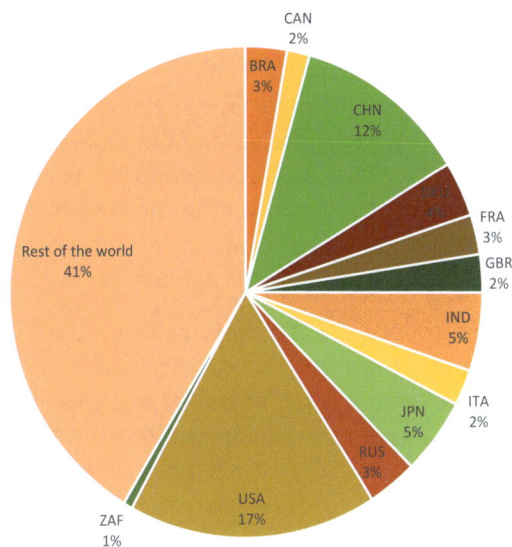

The increased exchange rate flexibility that China has decided to adopt responded to the goal of orienting production towards its domestic market. This goal has been pursued because the foreign market, compared to a production capacity that has tremendously increased and to an accumulation of private savings with a high inflationist potential, was becoming too fragile.

This meant that China, in the medium term, would have no longer been interested in financing the American deficit. This change, however, would take some time since there were concerns a rapid depreciation of the U.S. dollar could in turn devaluate China's dollar-denominated assets. In addition, Asia still lacked a sufficiently sophisticated financial market that could assure proper use of its savings.[61] In the following chapters we will develop further some considerations about what could be needed to ensure the conditions for China to open more its financial markets in a condition that ensures stability and prevents unwanted and uncontrolled capital outflows or inflows.

On the eve of the 2009 G20 meeting in London, where it was planned to discuss how the major world economies were managing the financial crisis generated from the United States, Zhou Xiaochuan, the Chinese central bank's governor, published a paper in the journal of the Bank for International Settlements. In that paper, the Chinese governor reiterated the problem of the impossibility to deal with global macroeconomic imbalances and assure financial stability without confronting the unsolved issue of the international monetary system, namely the absence of an international reserve currency pegged to a stable value.

Zhou reintroduced Triffin's arguments on the flaws of a system where a national currency serves, de facto, as a global reserve currency and declared himself in favour of a supranational international reserve currency, explicitly recalling the "bancor," the international currency unit Keynes had proposed in 1944 at Bretton Woods.[62]

Zhou's proposal was to reconsider the role of Special Drawing Rights (SDRs). Created by the IMF in 1969, SDRs were intended to be an asset held in foreign exchange reserves under the Bretton Woods system of fixed exchange rates[63]. It was proposed to foster the use of SDRs as a medium of exchange not only between the commercial and financial transactions of governments and financial institutions. Moreover, part of every country's official reserve should have been managed and held by the IMF so that market stability would be strengthened.

The Chinese proposal was not something new and responded to real problems. However, it was proposed at a time when the Second Bretton Woods had revealed its flaws and the possibility of a dollar crisis, with consequent value loss of the great amount of Chinese dollar-denominated assets, seemed real.

A year after Zhou's proposal, the issue of the international impact of American monetary policies arose again because of the Federal Reserve's ultra-expansionary quantitative easing, which had been adopted to counteract the recession.

Table 9

World GDP in 2022[64]

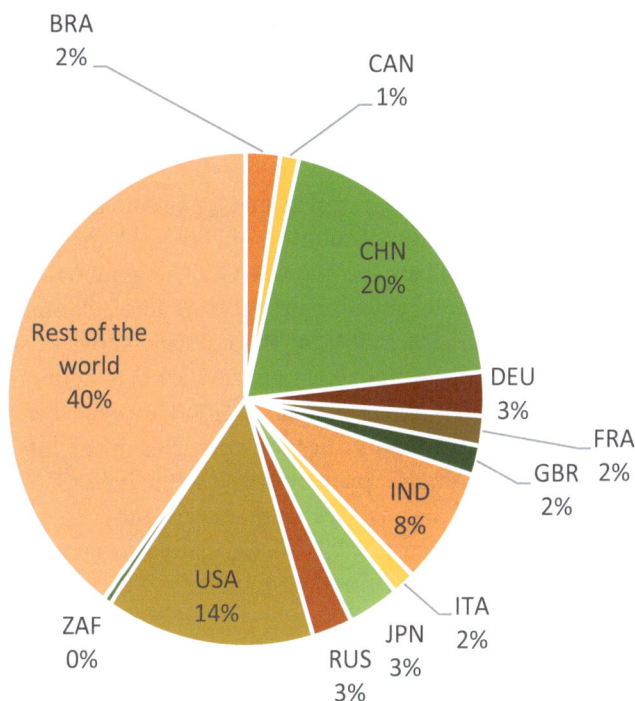

This surge in the amount of global liquidity resulted in increased investments in emerging countries—in particular Asia and Latin America—which offered higher returns. While in Asia, as mentioned above, China responded by pegging its exchange rate to the dollar and, therefore, avoiding capital inflows, Brazil was instead severely hit by massive capital inflows which triggered a rapid appreciation of its currency. Brazil was experiencing these capital inflows because of the strong performance of its economy, which at that time was commercially tied with China, creating favourable expectations regarding the external value of its currency.

The Brazilian government was unable to slow these capital inflows and, as a result, suffered a loss of competitiveness of its products due to the appreciated exchange rate. Moreover, its finance minister used for the first time the expression a "currency war" to describe what from its point of view was a foreign attack to the Brazilian economy. Although maybe exaggerated at that time, this military term would be used approximately ten years later by the United States (the issuer of that currency), not to condemn an aggression, but as a demonstration of deterrent power.[65]

In these ten years there has been a separation between the role of the dollar in the international monetary system and the economic global power of its issuer country. At end 2022, the United States produces about 25% of the World's GDP in nominal terms (but 14% in PPP terms) whilst China represents 18% of nominal global GDP (but close to 20% in PPP, so theoretically above the U.S.—see Table 9). Considering both imports and exports figures, the U.S. represents around 15% of Global trade[66]. However, the U.S. dollar remains central: one-third of the countries in the international system have a currency explicitly pegged to the dollar, 70% of global GDP uses the dollar as a benchmark currency, around 50% of global invoices and two-thirds of foreign official reserves and global external debts are U.S. dollar-denominated.

One reason for this phenomenon can be attributed to a network effect that feeds on itself. Since most of the trade is invoiced in dollars, it is logical to insure oneself with dollar-denominated financial assets and retain large official reserves in dollars to be isolated from the impact of dollar fluctuations consequent to American economic cycles and monetary policies. Emerging countries are, as a result, forced to use their monetary policies to stabilize capital flows. The conclusion of this analysis is that the U.S. dollar, which remains as important as when the Bretton Woods system collapsed in 1971 (despite emerging countries nowadays representing 60% of global GDP), would still be dominant even if U.S. economic power would further decline. In the following chapter we further develop about such idea.

4

Current Implications of the Lessons from 1971 Onwards

The collapse in August 1971 of the fixed exchange rate system established in the Bretton Woods agreement depended, as mentioned in previous chapters, on the fact that the increased demand for U.S. dollars as an international currency was no longer met by a supply of the same currency consistent with its convertibility into gold by the issuing country, the United States.

However, after the so-called anarchic period of fluctuating exchange rates, which was also characterized by years of high inflation and economic instability, the dollar has gradually, especially since the new century, reasserted itself as the dominant international currency both as a unit of account for setting prices in international trade, as a medium of exchange, with its prevalence in settlements, and as a means of preserving value because of its dominant weight in the official reserves of central banks around the world, e.g., as the currency in which much of the global debt held as reserves is denominated.

This weight of the dollar in official foreign exchange reserves has not changed substantially since the financial crisis of 2008 or since the pandemic. It does not correspond to the declining weight of the U.S. economy in global trade or as a share of global GDP (see tables 9 and 10). Indeed, both shares are declining in the

Table 10

World Trade (Import and Export, 1970–2023)[67]

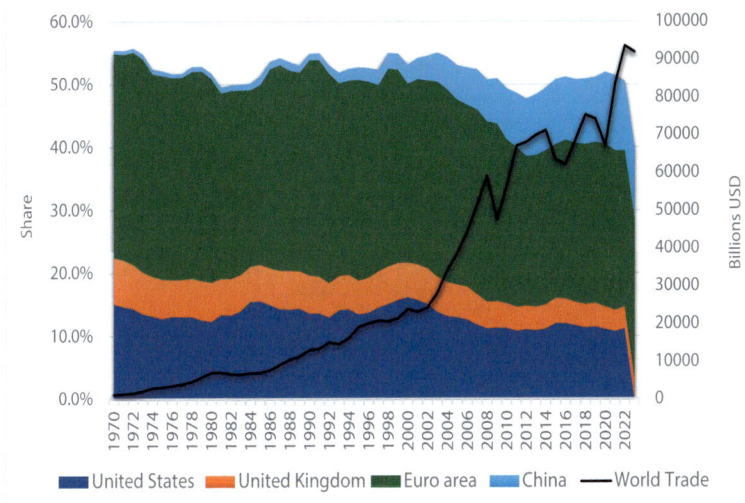

face of the growth of large emerging countries, especially those in Asia, with China at the forefront. Measured in terms of purchasing power parity, China's GDP surpassed that of the United States as early as 2014.

The divergence between the waning economic clout of the U.S. economy and the persistent dominance of the dollar as an international currency has been the subject of many competing explanations, depending on whether one looks at the dollar's use as a medium of exchange, as a unit of account or as a store of value—the main three functions of currencies. Obviously, these functions are interrelated, but it is of interest to understand which are the main determinants of the dollar's current role in the international monetary and financial system.

One explanation is that the U.S. dollar's strength as an international currency stems from a lack of alternatives. The Euro is not an alternative. Its share of official reserves remains stable at around 20 percent, commensurate with the eurozone's weight in international trade, but it lacks a federal government basis for issuing European debt that could provide an international safe assets alternative to dollar-denominated safe assets.

Table 11

Exports of Goods and Services in 2008[68]

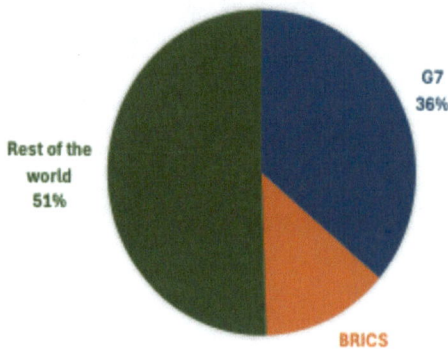

The renminbi, which has behind it a sufficiently strong economy in terms of GDP and weight in international trade, but still is not backed by its full convertibility and free capital mobility, is also not a current alternative to the U.S. dollar.

But it is also necessary to understand what function of money a future alternative to the U.S. dollar as an international global currency would need to provide, and whether a more multipolar international monetary system without a global currency is preferable.

It is worth asking, then, what drives the emergence of a single global currency and what drives a more multipolar system? This is a crucial question because the denunciation of dollar dominance can be motivated either by the quest for a global currency not issued by a single country (a modern version of the Keynesian "bancor") or by a preference for a multipolar system with multiple currencies to support international trade.

Economists have long argued that there is a convenience factor in having all international trade denominated in a common currency. Among the reasons argued by various authors are strategic complementarities in pricing.[69]

Extended and competitive global markets make it convenient for firms to set prices in a single dominant currency. These complementarities are also present when choosing the currency denomination of financial assets. Choices in trade and finance are mutually reinforcing.

Trade along global supply chains that interconnect many areas of the world has also probably contributed to an increase in the role of the dollar in international invoicing beyond the share of the United States in international trade.

The role of strategic complementarities in pricing and invoicing that goes beyond the euro area, in a period of global markets growth based on increasingly long global value chains, can also explain the increase in the share of trade invoiced in U.S. dollars even by advanced economies—such as the United Kingdom, Germany and other European countries, despite the growing European integration and the birth of the euro.

In turn, the risk attached to the prevalence of dollar in international invoicing amplifies the convenience of central banks to peg their currency to the dollar or to manage exchange rates to give stability to the value of contracts. This convenience is also shared by countries that issue so-called strong currencies traditionally held as reserves (pound, yen, and euro).

Additional risk considerations may also drive many countries to gravitate toward the dollar as a safe asset. Because safe assets appreciate in times of crisis, the dominant currency, which is considered a safe asset, is expected to strengthen its dominant role during global shocks and as uncertainty increases.

Table 12

Chinese Renminbi / U.S. Dollar Exchange Rates (1974–2023)[70]

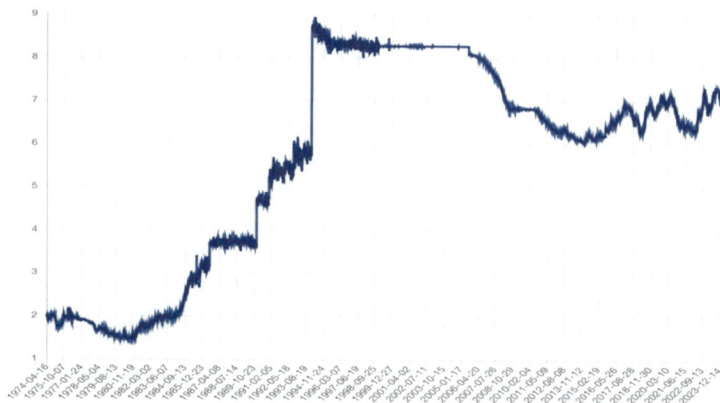

Source: Banca d'Italia

This means that the role of the dollar in international pricing drives its role in the payments system and, more importantly, it also becomes critical as a safe asset, that is as a store of value, in official foreign exchange reserves, especially if the exchange rate system moves toward "pegged" or managed exchange rates. It also follows from this that if a country can credibly anchor its exchange rate to the dominant currency, then it can borrow at lower rates.

Exchange rates have been more stable since the mid-nineties of the last century, although there were no true fixed exchange rate agreements behind (see tables 12, 13 and 15). The point is to understand the reasons for this higher stability of foreign exchange rates, which appear to be correlated to the maintenance of the dollar's dominant role, and not related to the decline of the weight of the U.S. economy in world GDP and global trade.

An important role in the stabilization of exchange rates seem to have been played by the collapse of inflation (see table 16) and the decrease in inflation volatility in the first two decades of this century.[71] This was mainly due to the liberalization of international trade, China's entry into the WTO, and an unprecedented increase in the global labour supply, as Chinese and East European workers poured into global markets following the end of the Cold War and the dissolution of the Soviet Union.[72]

The growing tendency of advanced countries to adopt monetary policies inspired by "inflation targeting" has helped reducing

Table 13

Euro vs U.S. Dollar Exchange Rates (1999-2023)[73]

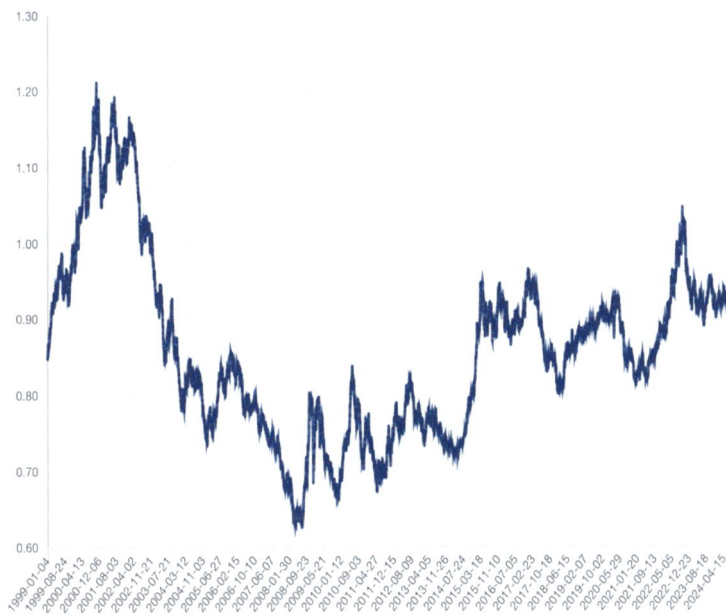

Source: Banca d'Italia

global inflation's volatility. These policies prompted most central banks to stabilize exchange rates, including manoeuvring interest rates, against an anchor currency, most often the dollar. Exchange rate stabilization has also resulted from the staggering increase in the official foreign exchange reserves of central banks, especially those of large emerging countries, mainly China, due to their growth in international trade.

The accumulation of large reserves denominated in dollars by these countries has been crucial in stabilizing foreign exchange rates due to the convenience of maintaining the value of their reserves and avoiding the appreciation of own currencies.

As a result, the total stock of reserves held by central banks increased about sixfold since the beginning of the century (from 2 trillion to 12 trillion dollars in 2020), almost 60 percent of which is in dollars. Although, as will be discussed in more detail below, the share of total reserves held in dollars has decreased since the beginning of the century, the amount of reserves denominated in dollars has significantly increased. This means that the underlying stock of U.S. debt has expanded.

In conclusion, the prevailing features of the first decades of the 21st century are the fall in exchange rate volatility even among the major advanced economies and the emergence of greater general exchange rate stability reminiscent of that of the Bretton Woods system prior to its collapse in 1971.[74] As noted above this is partly due to the decline and convergence of inflation rates around the world and the extension of inflation targeting monetary policies.

Moreover, because the maintenance of relatively stable exchange rates limits the possibility, in the presence of capital mobility, of monetary policies that would allow interest rates to vary independently, the lower divergence of interest rates around the world has been another feature of the last few decades that resembles the period of the Bretton Woods system, while the period after its collapse was characterized by greater exchange rate fluctuations and widening interest rate differences between countries.

Table 14

World Forex Reserves (1999-2023) [75]

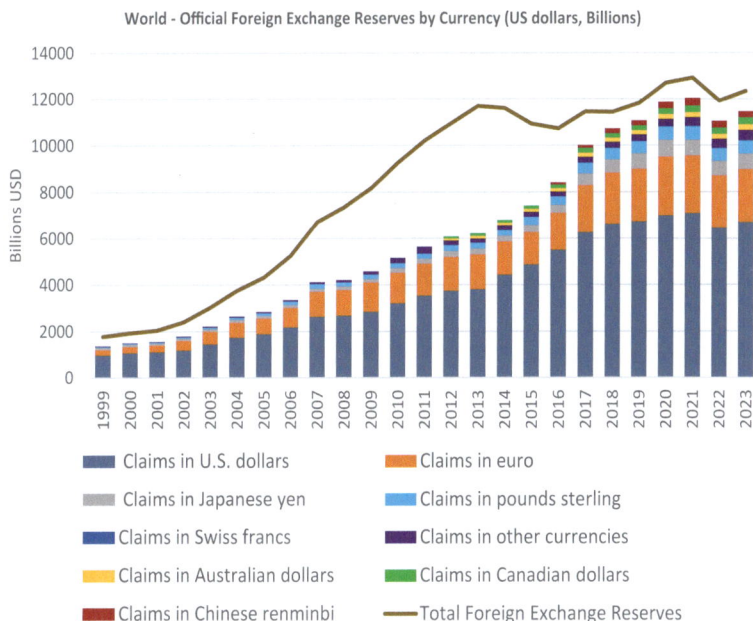

World - Official Foreign Exchange Reserves by Currency (US dollars, Billions)

Legend:
- Claims in U.S. dollars
- Claims in euro
- Claims in Japanese yen
- Claims in pounds sterling
- Claims in Swiss francs
- Claims in other currencies
- Claims in Australian dollars
- Claims in Canadian dollars
- Claims in Chinese renminbi
- Total Foreign Exchange Reserves

Sources: IMF Currency Composition of Official Foreign Exchange Reserves (COFER).

To summarize, the following mechanism seems to have acted. The environment of low inflation or deflation brought about by globalization[76] led to lower interest rates and less dispersion of interest rates among countries, and this put less pressure on monetary policies and on exchange rates and their variability. Monetary policies have, in fact, been geared toward stabilizing exchange rates and thus following the monetary policy adopted by the country issuing the dominant currency, e.g., the United States. This mechanism has been reinforced by the parallel decline of restrictions on capital flows that has increased capital mobility.

Table 15

Deutsche Mark vs U.S. Dollar Exchange Rates (1955-2001) [77]

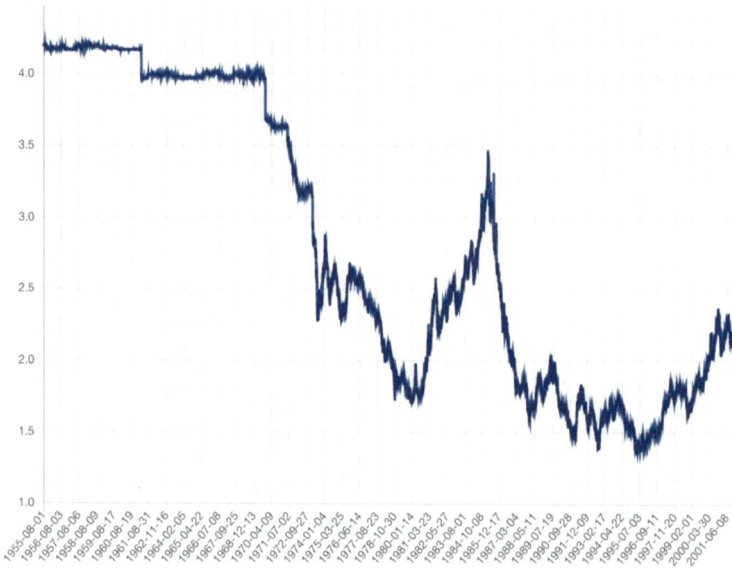

Source: Banca d'Italia

All this again leads directly to Triffin's dilemma, already mentioned in the previous chapters: you cannot have monetary sovereignty, exchange rate management and free capital mobility at the same time in an open economy. This implies that countries that want to maintain a fixed exchange rate must queue up to the monetary policy of the central bank that issues the anchor currency, which is, in the current system and context described, the U.S. Federal Reserve.

The practice of sterilization interventions can substitute for capital mobility control to stabilize the exchange rate, but this requires large reserves in the dominant foreign currency. China has used both capital control and sterilization and remains the largest holder of foreign exchange reserves. In 2020, China held about a quarter of all official foreign exchange reserves of central banks.

Table 16

Inflation in the U.S. (1944-2020)[78]

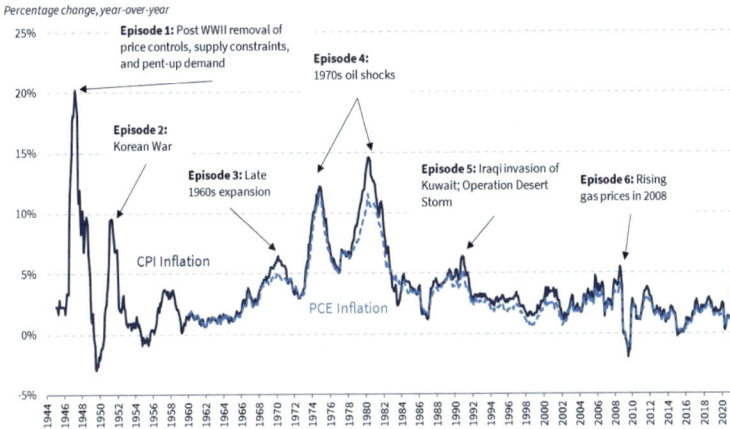

Percentage change, year-over-year

Episode 1: Post WWII removal of price controls, supply constraints, and pent-up demand

Episode 2: Korean War

Episode 3: Late 1960s expansion

Episode 4: 1970s oil shocks

Episode 5: Iraqi invasion of Kuwait; Operation Desert Storm

Episode 6: Rising gas prices in 2008

CPI Inflation

PCE Inflation

U.S. Dollar Dominance in International Official Reserves

In the modern version of Triffin's dilemma, the credibility of the dollar as a safe asset rests substantially in the continuation of the determinants that support its demand, not in its convertibility in gold. Therefore, the question that needs to be asked is whether the factors that have led to the de facto reproduction of the Bretton Woods system may change and what the consequences might be, and whether this system reproduces in different forms the inherent instability that led to the collapse of the first Bretton Woods.

In fact, the share of international reserves in dollars declined[79] by 12 percent between 1999 and 2021.[80] This suggests a possible gradual decline in the role of the dollar as the dominant international currency. However, it is necessary to consider the possible explanations.

This decrease in the share of global reserves held in dollars does not correspond to a smaller U.S. share in world trade or to a diminished credibility of the dollar as a safe asset, also considering that the decrease in the share of dollar reserves has not gone to other "traditional" reserve currencies (euro, pound, yen). It is rather more the result of portfolio diversification choices made by central bank managers.

According to some authors three main factors have contributed to this shift of foreign exchanges reserves to new currencies.[81] The first is the increasing liquidity of markets.

At the turn of the century few countries had markets deep and liquid to exchange domestic weak currencies, or assets denominated in their domestic currency, with other weak currencies (defined as non-reserve currencies). Therefore, in most developing and emerging countries it was easier to buy U.S. dollars (or Swiss francs, British pounds, euros, or yen) and then with these strong currencies to buy other currencies. In other words, it was easier to exchange currencies by using dollars, or to a lesser extent other hard currencies, as intermediaries, rather than directly exchanging the domestic currency for another weak domestic currency in the international market.

This difficulty of transacting between non-strong currencies is the basis of the so-called network effect. However, these costs and efficiency advantages of holding hard currency reserves, particularly dollars, have probably diminished due to technological advances that allow potential foreign currency exchanges and payment platforms between all currencies. In addition, the expanding network of central bank currency swap lines made it easier in emergencies to obtain hard currencies not held as reserves.

The second factor is the increase in the share of reserves held in excess of liquidity reserves, held in low-risk or safe assets, that is the amount of reserves that can be used for investment for a return. This phenomenon became more pronounced as bond yields denominated in the four major reserve currencies, including the U.S. dollar, declined, with yields trending toward zero. This third factor would steer reserve diversification toward nontraditional currencies.

These possible explanations of the decrease of the share of dollar-denominated foreign exchange reserves look at market forces and stand alongside official policy explanations related to both the so-called internationalization of the renminbi, even if only a quarter of diversification went toward the Chinese currency, and the role of the euro that would have led to a reduction in the share of reserves held in Europe.

But what seems to matter most is the relationship between pegging to a currency and the share of reserves held in that currency such that the exchange rate can be managed. In this framework the size of the economy of the country issuing the reference currency, or its weight in international trade, matters less in determining the share of reserves held in in that currency. What matters more is the demand of this currency motivated by the convenience of maintaining a relatively stable exchange rate system and the amount of debt that this same economy can issue as a safe asset while maintaining the credibility of its value. This is why dollar demand remains high, despite the growing weight of emerging countries in global trade and the lower weight of the United States and the other G7 countries.

On the other hand, too, the main benefit, "the exorbitant privilege," that comes to the country issuing the currency used as the international currency is to condition the rest of the world with its monetary policy and to have unlimited credit to support its trade deficits, because this unlimited credit is the condition for maintaining the exchange rate unchanged that is the determinant of the demand for the same currency. It is thus the demand for safe assets denominated in dollars, the basis of which is confidence in the sustainability of the underlying debt, that is at the heart of the dollar's role in the international monetary system.

The questions to be answered are therefore as follows: what factors may reduce the demand for dollars or dollar-denominated safe assets? What factors may undermine the dollar's credibility as a safe asset or the willingness of the United States to provide the international market with an adequate and growing amount of dollars, that is an adequate and growing amount of debt? What other countries may replace or join the dollar in this role? And then, of course, we must ask whether any reduction in the dollar's role as the dominant international currency is to be considered harmful to the Western world. The last question is whether the perpetuation of the current international monetary system is acceptable to the rest of the world. In the rest of this chapter, we will focus on factors that can lower the international demand for dollars, leaving other questions for subsequent chapters.

We have seen how low inflation and low interest rates have favoured relatively stable exchange rates due to choices of pegging or managing exchange rates that strengthened the dollar as the dominant currency. These may not be the characteristics of the near-future world. Beyond geopolitical instability and the effect of ongoing wars on the degree of uncertainty that prevails among investors, the rise in inflation rate may be a structural phenomenon due to the exhaustion of the globalization phase from the late 1990s to the present: the huge increase in global labour supply due to the entry of the Chinese and Eastern European labour forces into global markets.[82]

This resulted in decades of non-inflationary global growth because it allowed for low-cost production that met growing global demand. However, this phenomenon seems to be exhausted with the continued growth of the Chinese and Eastern European economies, and the great demographic reversal highlighted by Goodhart and Pradhan.

This structural deflationary factor is now fading and this effect is, moreover, amplified by market fragmentation and protectionist tendencies determined by the new conflictual competition for new global markets linked to the ecological transition (see chapter

5 on this issue). In a world with more structural inflation and as consequence higher interest rates, some elements of stability in the system based on dollar dominance are weakened.

The reason is that as long as prices are fixed in dollars, higher global inflation pushes all economies to increase demand for dollar-denominated safe assets to insure themselves against possible greater exchange rate fluctuations, and this helps keep exchange rates relatively stable. This means precisely increasing demand for dollars and dollar-denominated assets as long as they remain credible as safe assets. But this requires that U.S. debt, which is the basis of safe dollar bonds, also remains financially sustainable and not much higher than GDP.

It is a loop in which the very basis of the dollar credibility as a safe asset is dollar dominance itself. But this requires the United States to continue to issue debt and attract capital. In other words, the demand for U.S. debt reinforces its dominance and this pushes toward further debt growth that results in capital inflows that keep the exchange rate stable or pushes toward dollar appreciation, even in the face of a growing current account deficit and so preventing the adjustment of the macroeconomic imbalance.

On the other hand, barriers to international trade and protectionist policies, many of which are dictated mainly by geopolitical considerations, are ineffective with respect to the goal of rebalancing trade imbalances while they exacerbate the problem of structural inflation, which in turn will force interest rates higher than in recent decades and reinforce the described mechanism of rebalancing the U.S. balance of payments by capital inflows. But the stability of the system would be weakened if, in a new environment of higher interest rates, the competitive advantage enjoyed by U.S. dollar-denominated debt, due to the premium on dollar denominated bonds yields, is no longer sufficient to avoid raising the issue of its sustainability.

The impact of de-globalization and the trend toward market fragmentation may also affect the stability of the system based on the dominance of the dollar through another transmission channel as well. The shortening of supply chains and their delimitation within geopolitical perimeters may make international pricing exclusively in dollars less needed and consequently hold dollars as the prevailing liquidity reserve and safe assets as a store of value less appealing. This possible weakening factor of the network effect would be in addition to that resulting from the technological advancement of digital platforms for international payments and currency exchange that today can also enable a more multipolar multi-currency-based system to be supported more efficiently.

A final consideration, which will be developed in the following chapters, is that paradoxically the reduction in demand for dollars due to a more multipolar system could help to reduce global macroeconomic imbalances and progressively push the U.S. government to deal with the growing U.S. debt and trade disequilibrium.

5

Global Public Goods and Industrial Policy

There is a potential contradiction between the need to produce global public goods, such as combating climate change and preventing pandemics, and the drive towards the fragmentation of global markets for geo-economic reasons and even more for geopolitical reasons.[83]

Examples of this potential contradiction are the U.S. programs launched by the Biden administration after passage by the U.S. Congress of the Inflation Reduction Act and the CHIPS and Science Act, and the following debate in Europe about what industrial policy response may be required. The contradiction emerges if this revival of attention to industrial policies is framed in the context of Western discussions of so-called re-shoring, friend-shoring, or de-risking policies.

Globalization, in addition to the benefits it has brought, both in terms of global growth—which includes many decades of growth without inflation even in advanced countries—and in terms of poverty reduction in the world, has also fostered international cooperation in the supply of so-called global public goods.

Mitigating the effects of climate change or preventing global pandemics are examples of global public goods that require action across national borders and economic cooperation.

Basic scientific progress, the affirmation of universal rules, the dissemination of knowledge, international security and peace are all examples of global public goods, because they have the characteristic of non-excludability and non-rivalry in consumption. In other words, the enjoyment of such goods by some does not diminish the possibility of the enjoyment of the same goods by others. These are "global" public goods in the sense that their effectiveness depends on being shared globally.

However, the supply or production of public goods, and therefore also of "global" public goods, generally requires the production of goods and services that are not public. Clean air is a public good, but it is achieved through a technological revolution, a change in production processes and the consumption of cleaner goods, which in turn are not public goods at all. For instance, electric cars are not public goods, but because they pollute less, they contribute to the global public good.

The same example is given by the production of new drugs or diagnostic systems. They are not public goods at all, since they are characterized by excludability and rivalry in consumption. Yet they are necessary for the advancement of public health, which is a "global" public good because it increasingly affects the whole world due to the increasing mobility of people and things.

Likewise, while basic research and scientific progress can be considered public goods, their supply passes through the production of a series of goods and services that do not have this characteristic.

For example, research results, which are subject to patents or susceptible to patents, are not public goods but are, at the same time, essential for the public good that we defined before as "public health."

Therefore, the possibility of producing a global public good depends on the production at sustainable costs of these non-public goods and services and on their availability through free international trade.

This point is clarified by the example of the production of semiconductors and solar panels to produce renewable energy or batteries to produce electric vehicles. These complex production processes are fundamental for global supply chains and are concentrated in some countries today. Supply limits represent an obstacle to the development of a global green industry, and the achievement of greater production autonomy is considered a strategic goal in various parts of the world, including Europe, the United States, and perhaps China.

Similarly, in the pharmaceutical industry, over-dependence on production of components of the pharmaceutical supply chains concentrated in Asia is now denounced in Western countries.

We are talking about production of intermediate inputs, goods and new technologies, which are not classifiable as public goods because they do not have the characteristic of non-excludability and non-rivalry, even if their availability represents the new frontier of international competitiveness because they are necessary to produce what we call "global public goods".

The question, therefore, is how to develop technologies and production of these goods and services to an adequate extent globally to achieve objectives that concern humanity, which has increased from 4 billion to 8 billion in the last 40 years and whose well-being depends increasingly on the supply of global public goods.

This, in turn, raises the big question: how should governments support production of these goods? The answer is to be found by addressing complex economic and industrial issues.

The first issue is the relationship between localization of production and globalization.

The localization of production is not a neutral matter when it comes to the provision of global public goods. There are at least three factors to consider related to the intervention of governments in support of national industries.

The first factor is that national governments do not generally aim to overcome global market failures; this should be the task of multilateral international organizations. National governments want to support growth in their own country, make domestic industry more competitive, attract foreign investment, and improve the welfare of the national community. Public national interventions such as subsidies and public investments often have the implicit purpose of international competition rather than international cooperation and are often a way of pursuing protectionist policies. In other words, when competition prevails over cooperation, governments become more concerned with dividing, rather than expanding, the global pie.

This justifies the arguments advanced by those who warn that setting ambitious targets for ecological transition means, at least in the short term, favoring the industries of the countries that already produce the goods and technologies necessary for this transition and not the national industry.

This reasoning is superficial. It clashes with a second factor that should guide the localization of production, which is efficiency in the sense of minimizing production costs. This means localizing production where it is more convenient, also considering the costs of logistics, transport, supply of raw materials and intermediate inputs, and the destination markets of products.

There is immense economic literature on the advantages of free international trade and the exploitation of comparative advantages to increase the well-being of all countries that accept it. The private sector moves, or should move, according to this logic. The more it can enjoy free international trade, the more efficient it can be.

Globalization has advanced mainly thanks to the interests of private companies that have built global supply chains that take advantage of trade liberalization. Of course, some mistakes can emerge when the attempt to make the most of economies of scale pushes some to concentrate production excessively and therefore to increase market risks.

The third factor affecting localization choices is security. This concerns the production of goods and services, and related technologies, that are considered strategic in purpose (defence, health, strategic communications, etc.) and important to production chains, including mitigating the risk that such supply chains can be disrupted.

In other words, we have two security orders. The first is what we can consider "private" or "market" security, which has to do with the stability of the supply chain in the medium-long term. This problem can be tackled based on risk analyses and the continuous adjustment of corporate production chains.

The second type of security is often referred to as "national security." This argument justifies protectionist measures on the part of the national governments and subsidies to national industries. These measures distort the decisions of private companies away from the search for efficiency and generate trade wars and barriers to the exchange of specific goods, technologies, and scientific knowledge.

The interaction of the three factors related to the localization choices of the productions of goods, services and technologies leads to the discussion on the advantages or disadvantages of the so-called re-shoring, friend-shoring or de-risking policies that currently are discussed in Western countries.

Following these policies, we are faced with the prevalence of factors that are pushing towards a "geo-economic fragmentation."

The U.S. programs launched by the Biden administration, following congressional approval of the Inflation Reduction Act and the CHIPS and Science Act, are an example of the potential contradictions that manifest themselves in a push to geo-fragmentation of the global economy, paradoxically accelerated by the goal of ecological transition, which should be a global public good requiring cooperation.

These are programs supported by many hundreds of billions of dollars in subsidies, concentrated in a few years, and with the stated aim of rapidly developing an industry based on green technologies and the production of renewable energies.

This renewed focus on industrial policy to support towards the green revolution should be welcomed. These programs, however, have been judged by European countries as openly protectionist and discriminatory because many of the subsidies provided are restricted to goods, as is the case with electric cars, produced in the United States or with components mainly produced in the same country. The risk is that of determining a protectionist response in the same direction by Europe, where the discussion is how to relax European rules against anti-competitive national state aid. At the same time, we see increased restrictions on technology trade justified by national security in the United States and Europe and, consequently, in China.

The risk is that a period of trade wars will open in which the main interest of the various countries will focus more on how to carve out global market shares or win the race for technological hegemony than on how to cooperate for increasing the global production of what is necessary for sustainable development and to carry on the ecological transition necessary to combat climate change.

If this is the context of the debate, then many different things are mixed up under the umbrella of industrial policy and the goal of the ecological transition. We are faced with a fundamental global challenge: we must increase the rate of investment in all countries because the overall investment rate in the world has so far been insufficient to meet the objectives of increasing the supply of clean energy, accelerating the ecological transition in production systems, ensuring an adequate supply of food and medicine, and adapting transport systems—to support, in short, the life of a world population that has doubled in the last forty years.

China's economic growth has driven the entire world's growth. If today it has a quasi-monopoly on some essential raw materials, production and technologies for the green revolution, the aim of other countries should be to support their own production to expand the global offer. But for the time being there is no point in trying to restrict free trade of technologies and intermediate goods with the result of damaging world production in terms of efficiency and production costs and slowing growth.

In short, the paradox is that we are moving in the direction of a more confrontational world at a time when we must develop global public goods that require greater cooperation for a more peaceful world.

The direction of the competition between the advanced economies of the G7 and the emerging BRICS countries, leading the so-called global south, on the fundamental issues discussed above is closely related to the direction that a possible reform of the international monetary system and the future role the dollar, as the dominant currency, will take. Conflict and protectionism will probably weaken this role. It is worth remembering that wars are the main cause of change in the international role of currencies. The path of constructive cooperation for keeping open and free global markets is probably the best context in which a shared reform of the international monetary system, which protects the interests of all the countries, can be agreed.

6

New Monetary Tools and Possible Regulatory Issues

Recently, the Bank for International Settlements ("BIS") defined the "Central Bank Digital Currency" (or "CBDC" in a commonly used acronym), a tool currently studied by several central banks worldwide, as a digital payment instrument denominated in the national unit of account, which, as all national money supply (M1) is a direct liability of the central bank[84].

Given the fact that CBDCs are, by all means, de facto the same as the standard national unit of account (money), not only they embed the same features, but, also, must not be mixed with other private existing payment tools, and with what are the so-called "crypto assets" (e.g. the BitCoin) and "stable coins" (privately issued payment tenders based on legal currencies baskets).

In fact, whilst the former ones are "money", in the standard form of being legal tender for payment and a liability on the central bank balance sheet, the latter are equivalent to commodities, normally supported by blockchain technology structures. CBDCs do have the same value of the national currency tender bills, so are subject to the monetary policy of the issuing central bank, and, by definition, enjoy the stability and benefit of the trust that the issuing institution can transfer to money.

The difference amongst common "banknotes" and CBDCs is the platform, as the former are material (paper based) and the latter digital (so we might see them as "images" of the standard banknotes available on a digital tool, such as—e.g.—a phone or a laptop).

Current systems are still being tested and theorized, so CBDCs could be seen as a tool in development, which might have possible large "market" use (for the case of wholesale usage by retail users) or remain something gradually extended to intermediaries only, at least in a first phase. It is still unclear how this could practically develop, what could be the implication on monetary policy and on the "transmission mechanism" in the long run, as well as which relation there will be with private crypto assets.

This last point here seems very relevant, as many do see CBDCs as a way for central banks to take back the space occupied by new tools as crypto-assets and stablecoins and regain the full control and monopoly on the payment systems.

Recently there have been studies about the several forms CBDCs could assume, and the roles embedded[85]. In fact, wholesale CBDCs may be analogous to reserve systems, but could differ from existing real-time gross settlement solutions by making central bank balance sheet available anytime and exploring technologies that enable direct peer-to-peer payments between institutions.

A recent paper by Oliver Wyman Forum[86] suggests that "the launch of a CBDC would require adapting existing money movement rails, and/or building entirely new ones, and thus requires a series of difficult choices. This endeavor presents countries with an opportunity (among others) to reimagine their payment systems to fulfill a clear policy vision. Success will require being amenable to change as well as reconciling policy, technology and market impact." And that "Many central banks are at a stage in their explorations where the structure of a future CBDC system should be outlined with sufficient clarity so as to launch targeted technical experiments, while maintaining maximum flexibility to tailor the final system in line with public consultation, changing policy priorities, and the outcomes of technical trials."

But the question which needs to be posed is about money: will digital money become a global asset, not necessarily connected with the authority of a specific state behind, but rather accepted as a mean of payment based on trust considerations? Will the euro/ EU model, whereas money is somehow adopted and supported by several countries not forming a political union be successful? Today it is a hard to answer question: Whilst it is still unclear the real path that European union will follow in the coming years and, notably, if it will be leaning towards a "single market of sovereign states" or at least a partial political union, from today's perspective, the latter seems again unlikely.

It cannot be excluded that the spreading of CBDCs together with other forms of digital money, eventually largely used on international digital platforms as a tool to settle trade payments and transactions (at the moment it seems academic, but it is a likely scenario in the medium term) will possibly have an impact on the central role of the U.S. dollar as international currency and source of the "last resort" stability of the international monetary system. This could be a notable development only if such impact will demonstrate to be material and not negligible, as it could be a first step to an evolution of the international system, and towards the creation of international tools to settle trade payments aside from current main international currencies (U.S. dollar, euro, etc.).

But is there a possibility that the future of a global money might still bear the hat of the existing institutions, and particularly the IMF. Nevertheless, this seems still a far to be option, as would entail changes in the founding treaties which are hard to achieve. In such a case, clearly the role of the international institutions will be mainly the one to ensure that all the possible (planned or unplanned) evolutions in the monetary and trade system will be somehow respectful of the equilibrium ensured by the current "de facto" situation, with U.S. dollar centrality and euro and other relevant currencies somehow linked. Today this is an obvious statement, as it is evident to all players that even the ECB needs to consider its monetary policy options not just to ensure price stability, but also, at the bare minimum, to ensure that the euro exchange rate with the U.S. dollar does not impact indirectly, with unwanted effects, on the Eurozone inflation. And the same is also valid for all other main Central Banks. As such, we can say that beyond the appearance of completely independent monetary policies, the reality is that everyone in the World (at least the Western world) need to look at the FED decisions and take them into proper account when defining any monetary policy. Clearly, this "de facto" situation has benefits and negative spillovers for the Western countries themselves, including the U.S., which are in the uncomfortable position to represent the main stability provider, that they want or not, with all the consequences of this situation.

But, drawing from what Chinese governor Zhou proposed in 2009 or the revamping of SDRs as a possible "bridge tool" to create eventual alternative schemes to settle international trade payments, we will discuss hereby following why, given current rules, this is not a feasible option. Which will lead U.S. to discuss about the IMF capability to maintain its full role as the guardian of stability rather than imagining eventual additional agreements to fulfil the new challenges which we can see at the horizon today.

IMF Special Drawing Rights Allocation as a First Step Towards a New Economic Order[87]

The Special Drawing Rights ("SDRs")[88] were created by the International Monetary Fund ("IMF"), in accordance with an amendment to its Article of Agreement[89] in the late 1960s[90] as a supplementary international reserve asset linked to the Bretton Woods fixed exchange rate system.

According to the IMF's definition[91] "the SDR is an international reserve asset, created by the IMF in 1969 to supplement its member countries' official reserves. So far SDR 204.2 billion (equivalent to approximately 293 billion U.S. dollars at June 2021) have been allocated to members, including SDR 182.6 billion allocated in 2009 in the wake of the global financial crisis. The value of the SDR is currently based on a basket of five currencies—the U.S. dollar, the euro, the Chinese renminbi, the Japanese yen, and the British pound sterling".

The SDR was defined in 1969 as being equivalent to 0.888671 grams of fine gold, which at that time was the value of one U.S. dollar. However, after the end of the Bretton Woods system, the SDR was redefined as a basket of currencies. This basket is assessed every five years, to keep pace with the international importance of currencies in terms of their weight on international trade and on reserves held by states and central banks.

At that time, the international system, centred on the U.S. dollar, with all other major currencies fluctuating within bands (2.25 per cent and 6.25 per cent for the weaker ones), was still based on a "gold exchange standard" scheme, providing the possibility to convert the currencies of the countries participating in the system (originally established under Bretton Woods, and then realigned in 1963 and 1968).

Yet the market pressure on the U.S. dollar was rising, in part owing to the continuing imbalance of the U.S. trade accounts. There was a growing demand in the countries exporting goods to the U.S., which were paid in dollars, to convert these dollars into gold, and to repatriate part of the reserves held in the U.S.. This caused growing tension, which alarmed the U.S. authorities as there was a concrete risk of a crisis for the dollar.

In fact, none of this was unexpected, as a few years before, Jacques Rueff, the economic adviser to President de Gaulle of France, had suggested the famous "tailor paradox" to highlight the risks of a system where trade was permanently unbalanced, and the only way to sustain it was the continuing on-lending of new financial assets (loan or currency purchases) by the exporting countries to the one (the U.S.) which was the main importer of goods. Clearly the system, particularly as it was centred on the U.S. dollar, was only going to remain sustainable as long as trust in the U.S. currency remained unaltered and high, so that exporters were satisfied with detaining an increasing amount of dollars.

At the end of the 1960s, the international financial landscape started to change and did so rather quickly. Several countries, including France, Italy and West Germany, started demanding the conversion of U.S. dollars into gold, creating pressure that posed a problem of potential trust in the dollar as the main international reserve currency. At that time, the World was in the middle of the Cold War era, and such a development also had considerable geopolitical consequences. It was then clear that the Bretton Woods era was coming to an end and the then U.S. Administration (the Nixon presidency) understood that a new scenario had to be created to preserve the centrality of the U.S. dollar as the currency used globally for international trade.

Nevertheless, a last try was made to avoid the collapse of the Bretton Woods system, and that was the creation of the SDR by the IMF. The idea behind the SDR was to create a tool, open to all the member countries of the IMF (so not just the group of advanced economies), which could be activated by allocations decided by the IMF board and approved by members.

Such tool was not a currency, as the rules foresaw that it could be detained only by central banks and member states and a limited number of international institutions[92] —and not any private[93] entity or bank—nor was it a kind of "credit" to the IMF as an institution (as it involved a (limited) interest rate for the entities detaining SDRs, which was an ambiguity that had to be clarified immediately in the preparatory works).

Rather, SDRs were—and are—a reserve asset supplementing the international reserves owned by IMF members participating in the scheme (all of them are currently participating) to be used to settle international payments amongst central banks if the debtor country was unable or unwilling to pay by other means (hard currency, gold). In short, to use the IMF's definition, "The SDR is neither a currency nor a claim on the IMF. Rather, it is a potential claim on the freely usable currencies of IMF members. SDRs can be exchanged for these currencies."[94]

However, that also meant there was the possibility that, in the event that the counterparts (other central banks) were unwilling to accept SDRs, the IMF could activate a system to make compulsory the acceptance of such a tool to some market players—e.g., the most liquid central bank in terms of international reserves—which was supposed to purchase the SDRs in exchange for the hard currency then used by other central banks to settle payments. This "compulsory" mechanism was never adopted, and the few SDR transactions registered have always been voluntary.

The Crisis of the Bretton Woods System and Why SDRs Failed To Be Effective in Coping with that Situation

Clearly, in a certain sense, it seemed for a moment that SDRs could help to solve the problem of the pressure on the U.S. dollar and on U.S. gold reserves,[95] but it did not.[96] In fact, the first issuance of SDRs was very limited, and it was immediately clear that such a scheme would only have been able to relieve the pressure if the amount of SDRs allocated and available had been huge. However, whilst always concerned by the risks for the dollar, the U.S. authorities were also concerned about the possibility that a growing amount of SDRs, eventually transformed in a sort of international currency (which was never the case)[97] could have become a "new bancor",[98] thus acquiring the capability to challenge the role and the "exorbitant privilege" (although such a definition was not yet part of the debate) of the U.S. dollar.[99]

The outcome, as all the leading economists and observers were starting to figure out, was the decision of the U.S. to de-peg the dollar from gold convertibility in August 1971, following a deal with the Kingdom of Saudi Arabia and the main international oil producers to maintain the U.S. dollar as the only currency for trading oil. Such a move preserved the international role of the dollar, as all countries were forced to keep reserves in this currency to ensure their oil imports, but it also had a few other significant consequences.

The first consequence was, de facto, the collapse of the Bretton Woods system in the period between 1971 and 1973, as all the other

main international currencies had to be de-pegged from convertibility into gold and forced into a floating exchange rate regime. So,
basically, in less than two years from the August 1971 decision, no
currency was still convertible into gold, and the value of a currency
just reflected the market trade rules, as currencies were needed to
settle import/export payments, and the value of each international
currency was mainly determined by the export capacity of a country rather than by its need to import goods and raw materials.[100]
Needless to say, European countries had to bring in a new scheme
(the European Monetary System—"EMS") which mirrored, from a
continental perspective, and with no gold involved, the old Bretton
Woods system.

Another consequence was the sudden, significant, number of
U.S. dollars increasingly detained by oil exporting countries (which
were rallying in the OPEC), which also caused a significant imbalance. In fact, being aware of the strength that was given them
by the deal with the U.S. Administration and the dominant market
position of OPEC countries, they were able to decide to raise oil
prices by 600% in 1973, causing the first oil crisis, and obliging
European countries and Japan to hold considerable/very significant U.S. dollar reserves (to cope with their needs), whilst the U.S.
had the opportunity to increase the international money supply
without prejudice to the central role of the dollar, rather, implicitly
reinforcing it.

Yet it was not just this: the oil producers had significant new
reserves to spend, mainly internationally, as their national economies (those of the Arab countries) were still to be developed, and
this allowed them to become, at least partially, the "new tailor" to
use the old Rueff example scheme, although the Europeans were
not loaning money to them, but by buying U.S. dollars on the international markets to ensure oil supplies, they were, de facto, also
favouring the Americans.

On the other hand, the oil exporting countries were also se-
lecting the countries in Europe in which to invest their surpluses,
and this also caused a distortion, as petrodollars were flowing back

mainly into the strongest economies (e.g., West Germany) but were evenly paid out by all European countries. Owing to this combined effect, in practical terms, the weaker countries in Europe saw a growing net outflow of financial assets to the benefit of the stronger ones. This forced some countries (e.g. Italy) to establish barriers to capital transfers outside the national borders, which lasted until the early 1990s.

The third effect was clearly to lessen the reliance on the SDR as a possible global reserve asset, to the point that the IMF did not generate any new allocations after the first ones until 2009. Since the financial crisis of 2008, in fact, SDRs have returned to the international debate, and some scholars see SDRs as a tool that could help to provide liquidity and supplement member countries' official reserves, without distortions in international trade, and to help in coping with the limits of the current international financial market failures.

For a relatively long period, SDRs therefore remained a possible tool, with an unexpressed potential, and were, de facto, not used.[101] Allocations were very limited and exchanges, all on a voluntary basis, were minimal; however, things were going to change.

It should be also noted that since its entry in the WTO, China has represented a major player in the U.S. dollar market, as it gradually gained the position of leading demander of U.S. dollars internationally, building up significant amounts of reserves denominated in U.S. dollars, and represented by multiple assets (from monetary tools to bonds to others). This situation, which is currently part of the global financial landscape notwithstanding all the moves on U.S. and Chinese parts to start a "de-risking" approach, means that China needs to contribute to U.S. dollar stability, in its own interest (a depreciation of the U.S. dollar impacts directly Chinese reserves).

Now, if we consider that the Western countries are, somehow, all looking at the U.S. dollar to ensure their currencies stability and their monetary policies effectiveness, the fact that even China cannot afford U.S. dollar instability gives to the U.S. currency an event stronger position today than the one the dollar had during the Bretton Woods era (1945–1971).

Is this in the interest of the U.S. and, eventually, of all other players? It is hard to respond to such question, but we can for sure say that everything seems linked to the capability of the U.S. to ensure that the dollar remain the safe asset that all the world wants. And this has a price also in terms of options for the U.S. themselves. Anyway, possibly China and other emerging economies would welcome a rebalancing of roles (which can be a tricky option for the Western countries), and this is one of the reasons for the growing debate about the governance of IMF and other institutions and for the new life given to SDRs after 2008, albeit we need to say that the attempt to change something was relatively unsuccessful.

The SDRs' New Life During the 2008 Financial Crisis and the Events of 2021

Whilst at the end of 2008 IMF role was returning to the one of guardian of financial stability, becoming again the institution charged of following distress scenarios by "programs" devised to ensure a return to full standing for those distressed economies in need of help, already by 2009, the IMF considered expanding its toolset of initiatives. On one hand, it was decided on an allocation of 161.2 billion new SDRs, creating a total availability of 204.2 billion SDRs. On the other hand, a renewed debate about the relevant tools for stability and credibility of money supply was in place, as it was argued that the revamped SDRs (still the same as in 1968 by a design point of view, so in use only amongst central banks and institutions but not open to the private market) could be also perceived as additional means to counterbalance certain market failures in periods of great turbulence.

In fact, several emerging countries were suffering at that time with supposedly temporary financial issues, regarding their capability/capacity to settle international payments and this seemed a way to cope with such problems, at least partially. Nevertheless, the debate about the need (or not) for an international currency (which the SDR is not) started to regain momentum.

The end of the financial turmoil in 2009-2010, together with the new stability gained by the advanced areas of the world (notwithstanding the issues in Europe relating to the sovereign debt crisis in those years), led the debate subsiding again. China seemed to support the idea of transforming SDRs into a kind of currency, by eventually allowing their transfer to the private sector, something that the U.S. and Europe were not ready to accept.

The new crisis caused by the 2020 Covid pandemic outbreak has once again changed the landscape, however, and the risks associated with the partial freezing in international trade caused by the lockdowns in several countries have regenerated the need for the IMF to facilitate sovereign and central banks in their need for currencies in the event of temporary issues.

After the suggestion issued by G7 in 2021, on July 9th, 2021, the IMF Executive Board proposed[102] a new general SDR allocation to members, equivalent to 650 billion U.S. dollar (which is the largest allocation in the IMF's history to date and since this tool was created) intended "to address the long-term global needs for reserves during the worst crisis since the Great Depression". The new SDRs allocation will be completed by the end of August 2021.[103]

The allocation value of 650 billion U.S. dollar is equal to around 450/470 billion SDRs at current prices. This amount of SDRs will be allocated to members in proportion to their stake in IMF reserves so, for example, a country like Italy, which owns a 2.67% share, will receive around 12 billion SDRs or 17 billion U.S. dollar or around 14 billion euro. However, given the SDR's peculiarity of being negotiable only amongst states and central banks, the real impact of any new allocation in terms of expanding money supply levels worldwide will be limited.

Some Considerations about Reform of the IMF and of International Institutions

Whilst originally the role of the IMF was dual, as guardian both of financial stability (basically the original Bretton Woods mechanism and solvency of the sovereign participants to its capital) and of trade, over time this condition has changed.

The role of the IMF in the 21st century was already becoming significant in scholars' debates before the start of the new millennium.[104] The 2008 financial crisis led the international community to rethink how the IMF could fulfil its mission regarding financial stability, and this had at least one concrete outcome in the shape of the significant emission of SDRs that took place in 2009 and was the first sizeable allocation since the establishment of this tool.[105]

But, more recently, the raise of cryptocurrencies and of alternative forms of payments (even if only projected and never realized, as the notorious "Libra" project proposed by a U.S. tech giant) has further challenged the role of this institution. At the occasion of the 2023 Singapore Fintech Festival[106], managing director K. Georgeva floated the idea that "the public sector should keep preparing to deploy central bank digital currencies and related payment platforms in the future". At the same time, whilst the first attempt to launch a Central Bank Digital Currency ("CBDC") from the Bank of China did not meet market expectations, it is well known that both the ECB and the Bank of England are planning to issue such tools by 2027-2028, at least in a trial format.

Will these changes cause the need of a change in the IMF structure? This is not yet clear today. In fact, whilst it is possible that the definition of money supply as we know if could be evolving, once the CBDC plans of main Western central banks are successfully achieved and accepted well by the marked (which means CBDCs becoming an actually "used" tool, as clearly the value of the euro or the British pound will not be anyhow compromised), it is all to be seen if a reform of the institution should be considered or current architecture remains viable.

In fact, by today's perspective, the main concern about a possible IMF reform seems, in public discussions, much more oriented to governance issues—such as to allow for emerging economies more "weight" in the decisions—rather than about new tasks to be added to its responsibilities. The complication, moreover, is that any substantive change in the IMF objectives and organization will most likely need a new treaty to be ratified by all its members, which in a growingly divided World could seem an impossible task.

The same is also true for the role of SDRs, as said, as the eventual idea to transform SDRs in something closer to a token or a quasi-bancor tool clashes with the original design (1968), which has set for IMF clear boundaries (non-transferability outside central banks and supranational institutions, and, by the way, the fact that a yield is allowed on SDRs), makes it impossible, for time being, to imagine new roles.

7

Is a New Economic Order Needed?

If the IMF fails to maintain its role, which strategic implications are possible for the U.S. dollar role as the main reserve currency, and what implication could come for the U.S./EU leadership?[107]

In fact, whilst the Bretton Woods system was meant also to represent a transposition into the new financial World the monetary system based on precious metals reserves, the monetary system that we start to see today shows a significant change (a step reduction) of the "reserve of value" role for currencies (with some limited consideration to the role of the U.S. dollar and the main convertible currencies which gained a "reserve" role more linked to their value as "reserve option" in terms of "trust" in the Western system), and, rather, growingly today money seems more a simple "unit of account" whose credibility once was at least guaranteed by the Central Bank behind it, whilst today it seems simply subject to market sentiment[108].

And this is valid particularly for different means of payment (e.g. crypto assets), which owe their credibility to technologies such as blockchains and not to authorities. This would be a potential leap forward if compared with Keynes' ideas on a global currency (bancor) and will pose the problem of the need (or not at all) of a regulating institution.[109] It could be argued that money plays a different role at present than in the past: the economy pervades every aspect of our lives. However, unlike in the distant past,[110] nowadays the economy, especially that of the advanced economies, is largely "immaterial". We accept payments in money today that has not been convertible into gold for over fifty years,[111] and we are making increasing use of electronic and immaterial instruments to fulfil our commitments. Nobody ever thinks about this, but few moments in history have witnessed such a global act of faith in human society as there is in the modern financial system. Except that we are not talking about faith (in a secular, modern world inspired by the ideas of progress this would really seem out of place) but about "trust."

Yet there is very little difference in practice. We just must imagine that the real god who creeps into our everyday lives has the image we are used to seeing on the banknotes we all accept for every payment, because he is now part of our lives. It might seem like a statement worthy of a movie, but there are certain aspects of the model of society and the financial and economic system in which we find ourselves that have surprisingly practical effects.

For example, we all know how banks work, and how they have always worked, e.g. even the soundest bank of course does not keep all the money deposited in a safe deposit box but rather exploits it to generate income, which is then used, among other things, to pay the interest on deposits. To simplify things, this means that the banking system is based on a statistical assumption, namely on the fact that only a fraction of the money held as sight deposits by account holders (a large part of the adult population, at least in Western countries) can be withdrawn. On the contrary, the most obvious (historical) observation is that most deposits remain, on average, at the disposal of banks, making their "funding" a relatively stable source of capital (excluding exceptional cases). This all allows banks to operate and prosper as we see them do, to the great benefit not only of their shareholders, but of the economy as a whole.

Nonetheless, a crisis of "trust", with a consequent run on the bank, could cause even the most solid institution to fail. It is, however, far less intuitive to consider that, probably, the same statistical model for aggregate behaviour that makes possible the prosperous life of the banking system in each country is probably also the model, on a larger scale and with some differences, that regulates the relationships between the rich and poor areas of the world. It also allows the rich countries, which are then also those with the "strongest", or "reserve" currencies (for example the dollar and the Euro), to possess a great deal of "immaterial" wealth that attracts tangible goods towards them from the less rich countries as well.

This might perhaps seem a trivial example, but intuitively we all understand that individual economic actions taken as a whole, driven by self-interest (the security of people's savings or investments), do not always provide for solutions for the general good too.[112]

For example, it is clear that a citizen from an emerging country prefers to be paid in and hold "hard" currency (dollars, euros and so on[113]) in exchange for their goods and services, given their "distrust" of the national currency and their belief that that "hard" currency provides them with a better guarantee If only one person does this, it is not a problem, but if everyone does the same, then the currency (and the economic system) of that emerging country is automatically penalised, because the wealth (not only the intangible wealth) produced in there will mainly be transferred abroad, in practice into the hands of countries with stronger currencies.[114]

This will also cause a general mistrust of "weak" countries to continue, which will in fact make it practically impossible to maintain any accumulation of wealth with weak currencies (which are often also "non-convertible" and therefore cannot be exchanged with hard currencies, because the central banks that issue them do not have sufficient hard currency reserves to guarantee this freedom to the people in their countries).

Perhaps there is more to it than that: many years ago now, at the height of the Cold War, strict laws were introduced in some countries against the "export of capital", a very similar phenomenon (which has always existed) to what has just been described: faced with the economic risks of a weak system, those who could, transferred part of their means to areas considered to be "stronger", but in doing so, they made the situation in their country even worse[115].

If we think about it, this is exactly what happens with the current account holders of a bank about which negative news stories are circulating: they go to the counter to withdraw/transfer their deposits, which speeds up a disaster that, if they hadn't gone to the bank (and, above all, without the combined impact of their various individual choices that alone would probably not be enough to cause effects and consequences), might not have occurred.

We could talk about a "market failure", or to all intents and purposes, about an inefficiency caused by information asymmetries or by misguided conclusions drawn by several economically relevant actors. However, we can only conclude that the market works just fine: it reflects the effect of the set of individual behaviour of asset and currency holders acting rationally to protect their interests and capital, and in this case, the bank's account holders. It is not easy to understand whether the bank really deserved to go bankrupt or if it was a "healthy" institution unfortunately overwhelmed by adverse events.[116] We just know one thing: the "trust" was no longer in place, and that is enough.

Admittedly, the aggregate behaviour of that bank's customers - far from proving the principles of the "invisible hand" of classical memory - causes a spillover effect that is detrimental to the system where those same individuals reside and to their fellow citizens.

However, we could also comment that it is not the economic behaviour of some people that generates a crisis, but rather the premise of that behaviour, e.g. the lack of trust in that economic system, that country, and so on. In the end, everything comes back to a concept of trust. We need to consider that this idea of "trust" in money is fundamental to any idea for a new scheme for financial stability (e.g. a new Bretton-Woods like scheme), which is the main object of this work.

It is precisely this trust, however, that is becoming something very different in the contemporary world than it was in the past, including the distant past, in which the apparently multiplying effect created by the behaviour of market operators had always been linked to forms of material goods or securities. Starting with the well-known historical case of the operations of the financier John Law,[117] which, not by chance, are considered forerunners to the spread of banknotes, and going on to the various crises over time, we cannot fail to see that the historical trend has always denoted a gradual relinquishing of "store of value" money (that in gold or silver or with an intrinsic value) in favour of new forms of payment that are less tied to an underlying security.

Indeed, if money were a "commodity" (e.g. more or less convertible into gold[118] or equivalent values), trust in the banking and financial system needed (and this was largely enough to protect specific and collective interests) the guarantee of the state and the law. This kind of support granted states a privilege, namely of being the guarantors of last resort for the economy. However, this also meant that politics had "primacy", and this primacy, which was originally based on the authority of the sovereign, itself of divine emanation, as was the rule in the *Ancien Régime,* was also based on economic models, ideologies and ideas in the period following the French Revolution which were then realised in concrete proposals for society.

Nevertheless, precisely because money today is no longer tied to any "commodity" (gold, for example), it is only accepted and appreciated based on market confidence, and because it is the currency needed to trade with the monetary area that issues it. In a way today, more than a claim on the central bank of the state that issues it (thus a "store of value"), it seems to be above all a payment instrument and unit of account for trade with that area (or with areas that accept a given currency, which in the case of the U.S. dollar and to a lesser extent the euro, is of course a wider concept).

We need then to consider that today the role of "reserve of value" did not completely disappear, but it is more significant for those holders of U.S. dollars or other convertible currencies outside the borders of issuing countries (so, for the emerging economies), as the holding of reserves in such currencies constitutes an "option" for possible international purchases (or trade settlements) which they cannot ensure by their national currencies. But the consequence is that the actual wealth represented by all circulating money is likely biased in favour of those countries which have the privilege to issue convertible currencies, which, in turn, are the ones somehow dependent on the U.S. dollar stability (so the capability of central banks to ensure exchange rate relative stability (or smooth adjustments) over time[119].

Independently by any international implication, the evolution in the role of money, which today seems to U.S. not only normal and obvious, but also a trend towards a further, increasingly immaterial transformation of money, also leads to an important consequence: at the current juncture, for the first time in history, we are realising that the guarantee of the state and the law is not enough to make a currency an efficient payment instrument (and we see this clearly with "digital cryptocurrencies", which are also not actually currencies from a legal point of view), or at least the support of "one" state is not enough, as the principle of market confidence also applies to states.

So, money has now essentially lost much of its role as a "store of value"? This is not entirely true: currencies such as the U.S. dollar—which keeps its "exorbitant privilege"[120] as the world's reserve currency—and a few others (including the euro) that spread far beyond the borders of the state (or states) that issue them, offer greater "degrees of freedom" to the holder than other currencies do.

This is why these currencies are still held as a store of value, albeit much less so than in the past and in an asymmetric way (more in those areas of the world that we would call "emerging economies", less in the rich countries where they are issued).

However, and without claiming to deal exhaustively with complex economic issues, we could also say for these currencies that the monetary policy of the countries that issue them (the United States of America in the first place) implicitly benefits from an effect like that of a bank accepting deposits/a bank's total deposits.

Why is this the case? One simple example is to link the referable spending capacity to a currency and its market. If we imagine a currency of an emerging country, it is similar in form to the currencies of advanced countries. However, it is often not easy to convert it into other currencies, or it can be converted but under very penalising conditions, and this sometimes happens regardless of the will of that country's government or its central bank.

If a central bank cannot acquire adequate reserves in other currencies because its home country is unable to generate a trade surplus leading to a currency surplus or, otherwise, to access international credit for various reasons (including credit restrictions, legal risks, political risks and so on), it will be pushed by the market (by the sum of the behaviour of the operators, including the citizens of that country) to make the currency non-convertible.

Moreover, since that central bank is in a country structurally incapable of generating surpluses, and thus cannot hold reserve ("strong") currencies, it will have little room for manoeuvre to remedy the situation. Economic theory allows the central bank to operate on rates (e.g. by lowering them, thus devaluing its currency and favouring exports) or on the quantity of money in circulation (by increasing it, with a similar effect to the previous tactic), but in so doing it also generates inflation, and probably creates an environment of "mistrust" in its own currency, with few ways back. Mistrust in the markets will further fuel a crisis, because traders will tend to avoid holding that country's (weak) currency or to immediately take it to the central bank to convert it into strong currency, thereby constantly depleting the reserves of that issuing institution.

Eventually, that central bank will likely be unable to preserve the value of its currency, which will easily become "non-convertible", e.g. not traded or exchangeable for other currencies on the markets. This is because on the markets themselves, all private operators (and then the other central banks), knowing that that country's central bank is no longer able to exchange its currency into other currencies, having no reserves or access to credit, will quickly refuse to hold it or to use it to carry out their trades and business.

This does not imply that, in its "fundamentals", that country's situation is so compromised, but the fact that the market (the aggregate behaviour of the various operators, from the smallest to the largest, who act rationally based on their expectations[121] of events they consider to be most probable—here it is the possible default in convertibility—in order to preserve their capital) "believes" it, is largely responsible for the events and their consequences.[122] Paradoxically, and similarly to the case of a bank crisis, the market's expectation of a negative event with respect to a state creates a situation of uncertainty that gradually accelerates towards the realisation of that event, which becomes almost self-fulfilling as a negative *fumus* progresses and has tangible effects.

As for banks, in states where there is a crisis, it translates into the need to restore a situation of credibility, with problem-solving initiatives that, in the current global monetary system, often take the form of an International Monetary Fund "programme", with at least partial and temporary limits on a country's sovereignty. Here too then, it is a question of trust, and of course not only that; it is not far from the trust that account holders have (or don't have) in their bank, with the difference that here we are talking about central banks and states.

In fact, a "crisis of confidence" has significant and immediate consequences (which may explain why the "programme" is necessary): if the behaviour overall of the actors in the markets denotes a total lack of confidence, that country (and perhaps its people too) will probably not have access to international credit and without it, will not have the currencies needed to buy goods produced in other countries available to them. Any creditor will see that a country with a structural trade deficit and without a convertible currency will probably not be able to repay it (it will have no way of obtaining a currency to do so, and under those conditions it will not have easy access to credit). All of this will further feed a vicious circle, less and less will be exported to that country (there would be no means of payment) and its economic system and its people will eventually be poorer and poorer.

It might seem trivial, but it matches the description of a bank failure. Here, too, most consequences come about because the growing perceptions of distrust escalate, just like a queue at the counter before a bank fails. Almost paradoxically, if everyone thought the situation was sustainable, even a country with weak "fundamentals" would remain integrated in the markets and its currency would remain convertible, because people would continue to give it credit: this is exactly what happens in the relationship between customers and banking institutions.

In the case of a state, however, there will also be one final and serious consequence: the assets in that country, denominated in a weak, non-convertible currency, will lose their "relative value". In practice (and regardless of the legal situation - let U.S. assume that all the legal safeguards for property are in place), the market value (in "hard" currency, for example) of an asset in such a country will be proportionately much lower than the same or similar asset if it is valued in a rich country.

This may sound strange, but it is not: it is intuitive that a coffee in a café in London or Zurich, for example, costs far more than the same coffee in a city in an emerging country (unless there are exceptional circumstances), as is clearly the case in the famous example of the price of hamburgers at a well-known American chain.

Now, let U.S. imagine that this refers to large properties or tracts of land: this would mean that the entire wealth of a country is valued less, proportionally, if its system and its currency are weak. In fact, a foreign investor who buys an important asset is aware that it is easy to do so if they use U.S. dollars for the deal (e.g. for buying a building) in a country with a weak currency. However, the day that they want to sell that asset, they will find it difficult to predict what the price of the dollar will be, and it might be quite a penalising one, or whether a buyer will be able to get dollars there, or whether it will be possible to convert the currency, and so the price of the good will fall because of this uncertainty. This applies to all transactions in general in this kind of situation, with a clear consequence not only for prices, but also for the real values of all goods in a country with a "weak" currency.

There may be various reasons for this (including legal, geopolitical and other aspects), but in the end, it is a question of general distrust in the national currency, the central bank and the country system. Conversely, if you are in a "rich" country, a parallel and growing virtuous circle is created, and that country will attract wealth.

In practice, to give an example of the two cases, let U.S. imagine a person from a "weak" country holding dollars, for example: they would rather continue to hold them (even abroad) than convert them into local currency. Why do they make this choice? Simply put, the operator is convinced that dollars will make it easy for them to access all kinds of goods on the market or to convert them into other currencies, whereas they think that it will be hard to have either of them using their country's currency. In fact, only in the rich countries, those with strong and convertible currencies, is there a real financial market, which also includes foreign capital that they believe—rightly or wrongly—can be quickly and readily liquidated from positions and investments in those countries and their currencies if need be.

The gap between countries able to have a capital market and those excluded from this circuit will eventually widen hugely, with the former able to polarise wealth and the latter impoverished. It is not so much, and not only, because of the responsibility of those governments, but also because their own citizens will try to save their own capital by investing or holding it abroad. Their currency, which is the unit of account for assigning a value to real national assets, no longer being convertible or accepted, will penalise the valuation of those countries' assets, making it negligible compared with that of rich countries.

All this might help to explain why a flat in an advanced country may be worth more than an entire building in an emerging country (if of course the legal safeguards there make its purchase possible and are equivalent in the two countries. However, if we assume this, the comparison renders the purely economic reasons very well). This behaviour is self-perpetuating (if everyone in that country thinks this way, no one will want the national currency and it will be worth less and less). Yet it is also a symptom of a market peculiarity that "reads the future" in the substance of expectations.[123]

Going back to the present time, it seems obvious to U.S. that money is transforming, e.g. its predominant function is increasingly that of a "unit of account" and a "means of payment" to the detriment of its function as a "store of value". However, this is all happening without any control and not by choice of regulators or governments. What Western central banks can do, paradoxically, is to try to link their monetary policies and allow implicitly for the U.S. dollar to increase its central role.

While even the strongest currencies are no longer held for the sole purpose of preserving savings—because of inflationary risks—in the years after 2019, we saw the emergence and rapid growth of a global market for certain cryptocurrencies,[124] which have been purchased with a view to investment and with speculative profit expectations.

The "digital bubble" has, however, also shown that holding legal tender is no longer sufficient to carry out in full certain functions that were previously inherent to money. If, up to now, it might have seemed that the latter was just evolving towards a shift in its role (namely its main role as a unit of account and a means of payment), what has been happening in recent years in the markets, and the potential response of central banks, e.g. official digital currencies ("CBDCs"[125]) is proving that the very concept of money has changed.

There is continuity in one thing, however: even today, the trust of its holders lies more than ever in currency.[126] Surprisingly, nowadays states are no longer the final guarantors of the system (or, at least, they are not the only ones and they are not sufficient to guarantee its credibility).[127] But they (their central banks) remain the main support for the stability of exchange rates. And their stability is what allows for convertible currencies remaining role as "store of value", particularly for holders not based in issuing countries.

Nevertheless, it is not certain how and if things will really change in the currency markets in the future, or, for example, if the role of the U.S. dollar will be reduced (which is one of the scenarios in the currency leadership race between the U.S. and China, but now, it would seem to be a remote possibility). Since they are long-term scenarios, it is difficult to make considerations and forecasts about them.

That said, what we are seeing is also the sign of a trend that is clear to everyone, which will lead to an evolution in the role of money and cash over time. Money will become increasingly immaterial and will therefore loosen its ties with what was in the past the final public guarantor (the state that issues it).[128]

This is because there is now much less "trust" in states, and in institutions, and even in the European Union itself or the United Nations (very different entities of course). The situation is such that the International Monetary Fund has been forced to launch "study initiatives" on the topic to maintain control of its "space" and role.[129] This is because one of the side effects of the creeping revolution caused by the crisis of trust in money and in the economic system is the possible emergence of alternatives[130] and also the resulting need to redesign the financial architecture that came into being at Bretton Woods in 1944.[131]

Yet if trust in the monetary instrument is so important, what conclusions should we draw from this? In the meantime, we should realise that the wealth of today's advanced countries is closely linked to the fact that their currencies (the euro and the U.S. dollar above all) continue to remain at the heart of the system.

It is also therefore apparent that the "unfought" war that has been taking place for some years now in the world economic system sees the clear preference of the emerging powers (led by China), and of the more backward/less developed countries, for a new multipolar system that the West cannot easily accept: a new post-Bretton Woods system, disengaged from the currencies that are currently the strongest, would downsize their role and value. Over time, this would create a system of trade that is no longer regulated predominantly in dollars and lead to the end of the primacy of Western countries' currencies, with the practical result that the wealth gap between the various countries of the world would gradually narrow, to the detriment of Western countries and to the benefit of emerging countries.

It sounds like a paradox, but the thing that most represents wealth today is an intangible set of expectations and rights (the idea that with a certain currency you will always be able to buy goods or to convert it into other convertible currencies) linked to our trust in the economic system in which we find ourselves.

In a future that now seems increasingly close, the more transactional and "privatised" this system becomes, the more difficult it will be to locate wealth geographically, clearly detrimental to the role of states and politics, but it will also "rebalance" the values expressed by the most reliable units of account, specifically by giving a higher value to intangible and easily transferable assets than to real, tangible assets (e.g. real estate).

Above all, since currency remains the instrument (unit of account) for determining values, if it is no longer linked to state systems, and specifically to the market economies of Western democratic countries, the implicit effect of a decentralised monetary system or, at any rate, of a new "Bretton Woods" that places a new kind of "bancor" at its centre, would result not only in a substantial difference in how international trade is run (the settlement currency), but also in a probable narrowing of the range of values of real assets held in various parts of the world.

In practice, without U.S. being fully aware of it, the use of currencies such as the U.S. dollar or the euro in the Western countries also means that the rest of the World wants to hold these currencies, and this translates into a general appreciation of the value of goods in the stronger economies.

It is not just a question of legal aspects and property titles. We cannot ignore, as already given as an example that, hypothetically, an average flat in the centre of a large European city is worth more than a beautiful building in a large city in an emerging country. Yet it is not only a matter of relative prices (the "PPPs" of the International Monetary Fund's valuations should be able to give a more accurate indication of the real "purchasing power" at local prices), but also a demonstration that a set of intangible considerations associated with the use of a "strong" and convertible currency makes what is denominated in that currency preferable to assets denominated in weak currencies (for various reasons).[132]

If we imagine that the international system no longer distinguishes between weak and strong currencies,[133] because international payments are mainly settled with some sort of new "bancor", perhaps a digital one, the (unintended?) effect will be to wipe out the implicit advantage[134] that the economic area with the "strong" currency (today, the West) had before the new system was introduced.[135]

In recent years, we have been witnessing a series of developments that seem to be casting doubt on the old Bretton Woods system, as it had been redefined after August 1971,[136] and specifically on the centrality of the U.S. dollar and of the currencies of Western countries, above all the euro.

Today, the primacy of the dollar as the currency for conducting international trade is not in question, and transactions not settled in dollars are mainly settled in euros.[137] However, if a new system for settling payments were to be found tomorrow, the scenario would change substantially.[138]

Given how much the Western economies have at stake in this scenario, the fact that the U.S. dollar is weaponised[139] by the Americans might seem like a daunting approach. Nevertheless, since it is in the interests of the Western countries that it remains central, any alternative that would reduce the U.S. dollar role would be risky for the advanced countries, unless well agreed in terms of how and when any change could take place. Today what we see is a clear tendency by all central banks, particularly the Western countries' ones, but even the Chinese are not immune from this trend, to take stock of U.S. choices or even to follow the U.S. in its monetary policy.

What might a future scenario be? It seems difficult to imagine alternatives in the short term, but if a new system parallel to the dollar were to emerge, it would certainly have a major impact on the redistribution of wealth in the World. Today it seems unlikely to imagine an alternative system credibly promoted by some states, and what is most interesting is precisely the need to use the term "credibly". It sounds like a paradox, but "cryptocurrencies" and stablecoins have proven (at least for a while, although they have also shown the limitations in not having a central regulator to support them) that they can attract a certain level of trust in the markets, eventually even competing with state-backed currency alternatives.

This established fact shows U.S. that in an increasingly immaterial and trust-based system, it is no longer only the legal and political system that determines the acceptability of a currency, because whether we accept payment with a certain type of currency or good (cryptocurrencies are in fact goods/commodities and not money in the strict sense of the word) is a personal choice and not a legal imposition.

Let U.S. not forget that behaviour determined by economic preferences (the example of people in a country with a "weak" currency) does not always achieve optimal results for everyone or for the system. Today there is no easy alternative that can cushion any divergences, because the world is divided and competitive and the decisions of states (slanted to their own interests) are not like those of partners sitting round a table looking for the optimal solution for all, and, if anything, are far more like the behaviour of customers at a branch of a bank in crisis.

Thus, the future of the economic system will increasingly be linked to the trust that the payment means we use can gain in the market. Now, there are no clear alternatives to the dollar and the currencies in any case linked to the system of Western countries. This also implies that the world's wealth will implicitly continue to be *de facto* "attracted" to rich countries, precisely because of the aggregate of the individual behaviour of holders of goods and currencies.

So, what could lead to a crisis for this system? Probably an increasing "decoupling" of the economy[140] and a rift between the Western system and China and the emerging countries will create major tension and, looking ahead, could also undermine the central role of the dollar. This does not seem very likely today, but now more than ever before in history it is more a question of trust than of concrete elements.

What would happen if, at some point, confidence ebbed away, and the behaviour of the markets was like that of the account holders of a bank in distress? It is easy for U.S. today to grasp the perverse effects of monetary mechanisms and, depending on where we are in the world - so probably if we all found ourselves in Rawls' famous "veil of ignorance" example,[141] there is no guarantee that most people would prefer the current monetary system - we can assess whether such a system is convenient for U.S. or not. Nevertheless, it is certainly not based on ethical considerations.

All of U.S. in the West are aware, in theory, of the advantages of living in a wealthy part of the world, a fact that seems obvious to everyone, but we are much less willing to realise that the economic system in which we live needs to evolve to ensure its own survival and sustainability.

This is not what happens, and not only because in such a complex system, but it is also not only the choices of public or democratic institutions that determine the course of economic events. Instead, it is often the market rules that influence people's will and preferences (the well-known economist John Kenneth Galbraith,[142] argued that capitalism is the only system where everyone has something to lose, and is therefore the most stable), sometimes with sub-optimal effects, such as the generalised prioritisation of the short term over forward-looking choices.

Paradoxically, the current system is susceptible to influences (particularly, of course, those of the "strongest" economic systems) but there is no way to determine its developments with any certainty (not even in fora such as the G7 or the IMF). It is perhaps precisely the end of the primacy of politics and the growing role of the economy that, more than anything else, has decided history the way we are living and have lived through it over the last 50 years.

Returning to strong ethical foundations in the founding values of civil society, especially in countries that call themselves liberal democracies, is perhaps the only way out of a growing uncertainty that is gradually turning into an apparently multipolar order but that, in practice, leaves many questions as to what the possible futures are. This cannot be a mere proclamation, however, but requires thinking that goes beyond a simple debate on economics, ethics and geopolitical balances.

8

How Can We Find a Way Out of Uncertainty?[143]

The Renewed Debate Towards a New Monetary Architecture and the Role for Money

The present time is certainly a period of great uncertainty: we are living in a time of uncertainty regarding the future of Europe, one of the richest and most influential areas in the world, we are witnessing a geopolitical crisis, which also includes wars but, much less visibly, also unfought wars, both in more "borderline" contexts, such as "cybersecurity" aspects, and more generally, especially in the context of the economy and trade.

This tension also leads to an uncertainty in the perspective on the international monetary system, for which new architectures (new "Bretton Woods" systems[144]), are now being dreamed up, and the central currency, the U.S. dollar, is the subject of tension or, depending on your point of view, of what we call "weaponisation".

Perhaps the most significant - and perhaps the least obvious in terms of common perception - aspect of the evolution of the world economic system in recent years has been the gradual reduction in the perimeter of the "sovereignty" of states. While a currency was once the primary mark of sovereignty (in the past, minted coins had a portrait of the sovereign, on the obverse or more often on the reverse side, and still do today), and only that currency was usable and used as a means of payment within the territory of a state, the use of a currency today, internationally but not only, is increasingly decided by the markets. In addition, what determines operators' choices is trust in one instrument or currency or another, not sovereign imposition, yet trust may be subject to moments of uncertainty.

In addition, uncertainty has a cost, and a very high one at that, because it makes it difficult to think in the long term and damages both economic growth and confidence. This is something that appears to be a separate mechanism linked to geopolitical interests, but it is the product of the behaviour and reactions of all of us.

To return to a positive climate of trust and to be able to look at the world again in a spirit of dialogue and peace, it is essential to get back to a situation in which there is a widespread perception of a stable outlook for the economy and for relations between states.

This very much depends on being able to find ethical values at the heart of human societies again, and thus also aggregate economic behaviour and, ultimately, by derivation, on stabilising relations between states.

Despite appearances, this is much truer than you might think, given the importance of collective behaviour that materialises from the set of individual choices, ethical or otherwise, and depending on what the dominant trends are.[145] In the end, if strong ethical values are widespread and people experience them, collective behaviour will no doubt ensue in a consistent way and any deviations from it will be limited and stigmatised. The rules of economics and politics, which seek stability in and the consolidation of their own situations,[146] will follow in their turn by promoting values that favour the common good, but also stability and economic prosperity.

This has been the case since the early days of history, and since royal authority used to seek the assent of divinity for its power. It is just that the perspective is reversed in the modern world, and democracy, which aspires to give (mediated) sovereignty to populations and ultimately to individuals, requires ethical values and the transcendent perspective to be lived on a personal level and witnessed in society, with ethical behaviour being reflected in economic and other choices. It seems like a paradox, but the decline in values has an economic "cost" for everyone and reduces the efficiency of the economy in general.

The Example from Europe

By looking at various examples, we can often find intuitive confirmation. Perhaps if we start with the current European situation, the extent to which the "credibility" of the current European construction has a "real" value actually escapes many people,[147] given that (and it is not just a question of the credibility of the central bank,[148] the context is important in the European case, because there is no state behind the ECB) the credibility of the European currency, the euro, and thus much of our wealth, depends on it.[149] Today the question is how can the European treaties be reinstated or modified, to the point that the debate, which will certainly not end with a simple agreement on economic parameters,[150] would seem to imply a reflection on Europe's possible future architecture.

This might sound like a debate that is far removed from reality and only followed by a few experts. In reality, this is not exactly the case: if, on the one hand, the potential architecture of Europe in the future will, in itself, have a bearing on what the future of European citizens will be like (and this goes far beyond the single choice between a future of political unity or with a simple, large market with common rules) on the other hand, the "credibility" of the system to be outlined and, above all, of the path that will be announced in order to achieve the chosen objectives (a bit like in the case of the "Delors plan" that eventually led to the euro) will carry almost as much weight as the theoretical goodness and effectiveness of the objectives themselves.[151]

To create a prosperous system that favours long-term investment, an environment of certainty is essential. Uncertainty has a "price", both in terms of choices (e.g. whether or not to invest) and in terms of costs: if the possibility of adverse events must be considered, people tend to try to incorporate their probability as a risk factor when making an investment, which has a cost, and the cost of the worst-case scenario is usually estimated. The higher this cost, the less efficient and profitable the investment, up to the point where an excessive "weight" of the various possible risks, e.g. the sum of their costs (or the cost of measures to mitigate them) makes an economic investment choice impossible, which is then deferred. Yet any delays in these investment choices, taken as a whole, impact (and reduce) competitiveness and, ultimately, the wealth of a country or economic area.

So it is that every step towards a clearer and more defined situation for the European union, especially those in the direction of a gradual move towards a clear objective of political union, will have an impact and a value, also in terms of stability and the ability of European countries to maintain and perpetuate the economic level existing today. However, today there is no clarity in terms of the outlook in this regard; on the contrary, expectations are often conflicting. One example here is the start of "European" debt issues under the NextGenEU programmes, which could have been interpreted as implicit and strengthened solidarity among EU members and the beginning of a journey towards an integrated European economic government, the first important step towards the creation of political unity. Yet tensions and divisions remain, and that instrument, which in theory is open to all member states, has so far been used very little (except by Italy), and this is certainly not enough to dispel uncertainty.

Even the fact that the European Central Bank maintained a very accommodative monetary policy during the years 2012-2022 to preserve financial stability, both by guaranteeing the renewal of the public debt held by the European system of central banks and through a large programme for new purchases, thereby acquiring a large amount of public debt of all the EU member states (limiting the cost of debt for all), could have been seen as a step towards greater integration.[152]

Nevertheless, it is not clear in this case either whether this was a definitive step, even though it is now difficult to "reverse" it, given the little leeway that the ECB has for downsizing its balance sheet without risking serious impacts in terms of financial stability and the real economy; this is why reading these choices as something that reduces uncertainty is not grasped by the markets. On the contrary, the huge portfolio of common debt currently held by the Eurosystem, and the ECB is almost seen as a factor of greater uncertainty, which shrinks the central bank's room for manoeuvre.

The European union is thus faced with the need to reflect on its future, both in terms of its architecture and the prospects for economic stability and, given the geopolitical pressures, in terms of security policy. The future stability of the European economy will also very much depend on the clarity and credibility used to define the new institutional architecture,[153] which could be political, federal or a simple market of integrated partners (moreover, we could say that a few, but clear, is better than uncertainty, in terms of the consequences for everyone). Any design will also have to be "credible" and trustworthy in the long run to make possible the desired beneficial spillovers (otherwise uncertainty would increase and so would the negative consequences).

In the United States of America, the strongly expansionary economic policy of recent years, pursued both by the U.S. central bank (the Federal Reserve - and this despite the monetary tightening in the post-2021 period) and in fiscal terms by successive administrations, has apparently not significantly impacted the U.S. dollar, albeit the long-term sustainability of such expansion is questioned by several economists.

American geopolitical leadership has been put under pressure in various parts of the world, from Eastern Europe to Asia, and this has consequences for the role of the dollar too. The growing rivalry between the U.S. and China could also be a significant factor of instability in the years to come. In fact, as well as geopolitical issues, the increasing tension between the two countries (and the blocs allied with them) could lead to forms of financial competition, including scenarios that are now seen as purely hypothetical, such as a "decoupling" of the international payments system, which could also have serious repercussions on the role of the dollar, and thus also on the euro.

Just as the euro has given its member states greater stability and a currency that is spendable as an international currency,[154] almost on a par with the U.S. dollar, the current international monetary system also seemed to have an inherently solid foundation, which the role of the dollar helped to make more credible. However, just as uncertainty about the future could pose a problem of long-term sustainability for the European Union, especially if there is no clarity about the possible political outlook, the growing international tension aimed at redesigning the global monetary system (the idea of a new Bretton Woods) is also a major factor of instability today.

In all this, the international geopolitical situation certainly does not make solutions easy, but if there were clarity over the long-term prospects, and this clarity had solid shared foundations that make these prospects credible, then even tense situations between states would probably be easier to smooth out and peace would be closer to hand. In fact, the main "side effects" of the uncertain situation are probably that tension in many areas of the world is no longer dormant and the difficulty in finding solutions. One of the reasons for this difficulty is that the lack of a long-term, credible and trustworthy frame of reference leads to "navigation by sight" by the main international players (not only politicians), with the ensuing drifting there for all to see.

The emphasis on looking at the short term comes at a great cost, because it has an immediate impact on investments (which are reduced in the face of greater risks if only because greater uncertainty is expected), thereby reducing the potential for economic growth and creating a growing expectation of further negative events. This spiral must be reversed, and confidence must be rebuilt to look positively at the long term again, and to be able to rethink our future in a sustainable and efficient way at global level.

So, what is probably the real problem in trying to understand future trends can be summed up in one word: "trust". As a matter of fact, trust is essential for building a stable economic and geopolitical future, and it underpins the credibility and stability of economic systems and thus their sustainability, both in geopolitical terms—since where there is increasing growth and wealth, consensus towards states grows—and in terms of the perception of the future (e.g. environmental protection or greater social justice). In the current context, trust is becoming increasingly scarce, and this has important consequences, in the short term, but above all in the long term.

For instance, the lack of trust is leading to increasingly short-term decisions and perspectives, with a growing reluctance of the private sector, especially in Western countries, to plan major medium- and long-term investments and programmes without at least a partial public guarantee or public support. Yet this is leading to a growing "market failure": while in the past, for example, the main problem for supervisory authorities, such as the anti-trust authorities, was to prevent the state giving distortive support to private economic actors (except where the market was incapable of freely allowing the achievement of public interest objectives), nowadays this line has become blurred, and there is an increasing need for public support for investments, without which they would not be realised, also because of excessive risks and uncertainties.

Compared with the past, therefore, there is now the objective problem of rebuilding trust in the market system and in the ability of institutions to provide sufficient protection from uncertainty to guarantee the levels of economic growth that have always been in line with the expectations for advanced countries.

This trust is not something that can come by political decision or by the decree of some authority, rather, it requires a return to values experienced in more of a micro context, from the ground up, as shared values as basis for looking to the future with confidence and hope again. From a purely economic point of view, therefore, we cannot fail to note that it is worth reshaping the model of our democratic societies in such a way as to revive the search for higher values as a guide to our personal life prospects.

This is because it is only a set of ethically inspired behaviours that reconstruct a need to look to the long term (and not to the short-term horizon of market events) that can give public and private institutions the stability and prestige that are essential for social commitment. This will also give new strength to the economy with concrete impacts that everyone can see.

This may all sound vague and not very credible, and far removed from the concrete nature of the economy, but it is precisely the economy, as it becomes increasingly immaterial and linked to trust and credibility, which teaches U.S. that everything that contributes to that trust is a multiplier of value. Almost paradoxically, we should resume looking within ourselves for those values that can then give strength and stability to the social and economic context in which we live.

Conclusion

What New Economic Order Is Awaiting Us?

The Renewed Debate: the Dollar and its Exorbitant Privilege

Eighty years ago, the decision to create a system centred on the U.S. dollar rather than to establish a multilateral currency (the bancor) was not just the dawn of U.S. leadership in the international monetary system. It was also the moment when the "old" pure gold standard scheme was buried.

In the nineteenth century and until the First World War, the international financial system was based on the full convertibility of currencies, which was basically very similar to a "bancor deal" but without the appearance of a single currency. The example of the Latin Monetary Union is enlightening: the appearance of the currency was to have liras minted in Italy or francs minted in France or Switzerland, etc., but the substance was that 20 liras were equivalent to 20 francs etc., so it was basically the same thing, and the underlying value was determined by an equivalent amount (weight) of gold or silver (in pre-defined proportions) in the coins. Only, the theoretical "legal circulation" of money remained linked to the national territories of issuing states, in particular for the tender notes).

Historically the gold and silver content of minted coins was the equivalent of their commodity value. Yet when tender notes (banknotes) started to circulate, anchored to a pure gold exchange standard (first attempts date back to the seventeenth century, but the nineteenth century was the tipping point), it was soon apparent that the coins in precious metals would have to be withdrawn from circulation.

If in the nineteenth century the UK could afford to keep basically fixed exchange rates and a global "gold standard," as trade was basically with its colonies at preferred (uneven) conditions, and monetary equilibrium was clearly something different from how we see it in modern economic theory, the relations among states started to change. In fact, markets started to show growing demand for banknotes, both for owner preferences, as normally they wanted to keep gold coins and spend paper money equivalent, and for external factors, such as the needs of the countries to expand the money supply for military expenses and other exogenous purposes.

All this soon led to an evolution to what we know as the gold exchange standard systems (so the possibility to redeem a banknote at its issuer either for its gold equivalent or for equivalent convertible banknotes, but denominated in a different currency), and, consequently, to a growing money supply. This evolution, which started to take stock of differentiations among monetary areas (e.g. for trade imbalances), led, in turn, to currencies that better reflected differences in trade surpluses and deficits. In the end, the result was a growing need to find an anchor for the value of money.

The two world wars caused further changes. When the allies discussed at Bretton Woods the contours of a post-World War II monetary system, the UK, represented by John Maynard Keynes, sought to put the pound in a position to be able to partner in a multipolar world. The UK did not want the pound de facto subordinated to the U.S. dollar, which in the end it was, due to U.S. negotiator Harry Dexter White's success in achieving a U.S. dollar-centred system.

It may not have been clear at the time that the Bretton Woods agreement accorded to the U.S. dollar its "exorbitant privilege." Many—including Keynes—could have thought that the situation would have evolved once the European economies had recovered from the war's destruction. But when the United States in August 1971 decided to de-peg its currency from gold, there was no question that the U.S. dollar was the centre of the international system, a position Washington was determined to keep, and that was further enhanced during the 1970s due to successive oil crises.

Was this bad news for the Europeans? Not necessarily: the fact that the U.S. dollar was free from any peg to gold implicitly "forced" West European countries to follow the same path. All advanced economies de-pegged their currencies over the next two years, so that by 1973 basically all currencies in the world had de-pegged from gold exchange standards. This was not just a step change from an historical consolidated standard (money needed to be equivalent to a commodity—gold or silver—to be accepted and trusted), it also implied several important changes in the relationship between monetary areas in the world and with the United States.

On the one hand, Europe and the other OECD countries were hit by the oil crises and their inflationary consequences. But while the United States could print as many dollars as needed, at least theoretically, other countries needed to hold them in reserve and to increase their exports to the United States to get further reserves. Nevertheless, on the other hand, prices of real assets in the United States and in the advanced economies started to be denominated in currencies which were demanded beyond their borders.

In simple words, before 1971 actors in emerging countries had the option to hold any "convertible" currency that was backed by a central bank with stable gold reserves. After 1971 they had to maintain reserves in U.S. dollars, which meant the need to have a positive trade balance with the United States.

The United States gained the most. But other advanced economies also benefited. The clearest example happened during the oil crises, when the surplus dollars held by OPEC exporters ended up being largely "petrodollars" held in Europe, with Gulf oil producers making large investments in Western European economies (and becoming relevant subscribers of their bonds).

As we explained in the third and fourth chapter of this book, what emerged from the Bretton Woods conference was intentionally not a "neutral" system on a global scale (the equivalent of a pure gold standard or of the theoretical "bancor"), as U.S. dollar leadership paved the way for the United States to dominate international trade (also to the benefit of all the West). Not even the 2008 financial crisis undermined the central role of the U.S. dollar, which has been confirmed as a safe asset, especially in circumstances of major international strain.

However, after 80 years and in a completely different world, the debate between Keynes and White on the utility of a global currency, the "bancor," has re-emerged, particularly because in a post-Covid-19 world there will be the need to redesign a new economic world order able to ensure cooperation between nations. The debate on the international monetary system and the role of the U.S. dollar was revamped already before the Covid-19 crisis, essentially in connection with the so-called "tariff war" between the United States and China, which represented a more general strategic and geopolitical clash. Three major factors have influenced the resumption of this debate.

The first factor is China's enhanced economic growth and its role in international trade compared to two decades ago. Connected to this evolution is the debate on a possible retreat from hyper-globalization and, particularly, on "decoupling"/"derisking" as a strategy to respond to the Chinese technological and economic challenge.

The second factor is the use, new in form but not in substance, of the dominant position of the U.S. dollar in the international payments system and in the international financial infrastructures with the aim to expand U.S. influence in extraterritorial areas and in pursuit of geopolitical goals. This phenomenon, defined as the "weaponization" of the dollar, or using the dollar as a strategic political weapon, raises questions and concerns for investors regarding confidence in the dollar as a safe asset.[155]

The third factor, possibly representing the major element of discontinuity with the past, is technology. Technology today offers new, efficient solutions for the payments system and, with the emergence of digital currencies and crypto currencies, reiterates anew the technical, although not yet political viability, of global currencies that recall the Keynesian idea of a supranational currency able to solve factors that cause instability and that are connected to the use of a national currency as an international one.

The evolving debate seems to send U.S. a message. "De-risking"/"decoupling" policies are leading emerging countries to hold more "diversified" reserve portfolios and have shrunk the role of the U.S. dollar and the euro. The result is a strange landscape.

Today the U.S. dollar is still very central; the stability of the system is still based on the dollar as a "balancing tool." Gradually, however, different areas in the world are creating economic ties less dependent on the dollar.

The eurozone needs to keep monetary policies aligned with U.S. policies. China, still not fully integrated with global financial markets, and with a currency that de facto is not convertible, must react to U.S moves, given the large quantity of U.S. assets held by Chinese operators. Even major oil producers, aware of their lower relevance given U.S. energy independence, remain essentially "dollarized" economies.

But there are some significant "elephants in the room." The first relates to China's economic size. How long can China afford to remain outside global financial markets by not giving Chinese citizens the option to freely convert their renminbi and hold assets from all over the world? It is something that must be considered wisely by the Chinese authorities, since renminbi convertibility could lead to unintended and uncontrolled consequences, instability, and risks for China itself. Nonetheless, that would be the real game changer—integrating into global financial markets an economy that in PPP terms is now bigger than the United States. This would also make the huge savings of Chinese citizens and growing Chinese debt available to global markets as potential new global safe assets.

Another issue might arise from the uncontrolled and unregulated market of cryptocurrencies such as BitCoins. These "currencies," which are only commodities, topped over 3 trillion U.S. dollars in value in 2024—sizeable enough to influence the stability of global monetary markets and possibly representing a payment alternative to national currencies.

Also CBDCs could be potential game changer. Their concept is not yet proven. After China's experiment around 2021, now both the European Central Bank and the Bank of England are proposing CBDCs. Should they succeed in creating suitable alternative mechanisms for retail payments (other than paper money and credit cards), the new digital euro and the digital British pound will each have the stability of the backing of a central bank, unlike BitCoins or private stablecoins. In particular, the digital pound, which the Bank of England is designing as an international currency that could be used worldwide, could represent a significant challenge to the world's monetary architecture, perhaps even leading to its restructuring

With these considerations in mind, we need to assess and understand how common interests could be affected by these three "elephants" (and others) and imagine how future scenarios might evolve and what that might mean for the world's financial architecture. Focusing on "common interests" means trying to imagine what might be possible and what will need to be discussed internationally. It also means considering both threats and global common goods.[156]

As we elaborate in chapter 6, we must also properly consider the fact that global monetary market stability tends to rely upon the U.S. Federal Reserve. When determining their monetary policy options, the ECB and all other main central banks need to consider not just their goal to ensure price stability. They also need to ensure that their own currencies exchange rate with the U.S. dollar does not generate unwanted inflationary effects. Despite the appearance of independent monetary policies, the reality is that Western countries need to take Fed decisions into account when conducting monetary policy.

As a paradox, even China is in a similar situation. In fact, since China entered the WTO its demand for U.S. dollars has generated significant dollar-denominated reserves. Notwithstanding U.S. and Chinese efforts to "de-risk," China has its own interest in dollar stability, since dollar depreciation directly affects Chinese reserves and the competitiveness of Chinese exports. The U.S. dollar continues to be the main provider of stability in a system with embedded instability (see chapter 4). Therefore, we suggest that the current international landscape might lead to two likely options.

Some Ideas for the Future

One feasible option is simply to allow markets to self-regulate and continue their current pathway, given that the U.S. dollar remains at the centre of the system and that Western banks and even China have an interest in dollar stability. The difficult question under this scenario is whether over the long term the United States can sustain the dollar's role of last-resort provider of safe assets by continuing to increase public debt and the money supply.

Should geopolitical tensions combine with economic pressures generated by private money or "de-risking" policies, then the United States and Western countries would have an interest in imagining a scenario in which they strike some international agreements to mitigate risks of instability and prevent a collapse of the system.

This second scenario, which is premised on the assumption that markets tend to find equilibrium, would entail the creation of new international fora underpinned by common rules designed to ensure monetary stability in the face of potential challenges posed by private alternatives to money or by CBDCs.

Under this scenario we might imagine the negotiating path that would be needed to hammer out a new Bretton Woods-type global agreement. This agreement should have two correlated purposes. First, the dollar's role as a global currency must be compatible with the stability of the international monetary system itself. Second, the "exorbitant privilege" currently enjoyed by the United States must be compatible with mechanisms needed to correct macroeconomic imbalances. This means dealing with the Triffin dilemma.

The option of a "bancor-like" international monetary tool could also be considered. It would need to pass the market test as a credible alternative to the dollar. It might be introduced as a side option to the existing system, to reduce eventual pressures on U.S. dollars while retaining the role of the U.S. currency.

The goal should be to move towards a more multipolar system without giving up the possibility of having a global anchor currency, albeit one that is not a national currency issued by a single country. In the current context of international relations and related geo-economic and geopolitical tensions, it is difficult to imagine this. What can be designed is a possible path towards a gradual correction of the system, although a possible goal should be shared.

A possible successful example of the past is the pathway created by the "Delors Plan" to achieve the result to facilitate the establishment of the euro[157].

Table 17

The three phases of the European Monetary Union

First phase (1990-94)	• Complete freedom of capital flows • Strengthening of cooperation between central banks and free use of the ECU (European unit of account, later replaced by the euro) • Improvement of economic convergence
Second phase (1994-98)	• From the 1st Jan. 1994, creation of the European Monetary Institute (IME) • Reinforcement of economic convergence • Progressive realization of the independence of the national central banks, to be completed at the latest by the date of establishment of the European System of Central Banks. Ban on public sector financing by central banks. Increased coordination of monetary policies
Third phase (after 1999)	• 1st Jan. 1999 : Irrevocable fixing of conversion rates. Euro introduction • Conduction of the single monetary policy by the European System of Central Banks • Implementation of the new European Exchange Agreements (EEA II) • Implementation of the Stability and Growth Pact

That scheme led to the euro because it represented a reasonable compromise in terms of the national interests of the main European countries. To achieve a similar result on a global scale, one should carefully consider whether this method would be a possible option or whether current trends might lead to an acceptable equilibrium.

We do believe that eventual compromises will need to be grounded in a sufficient level of common interest by all participants. On the following page we propose a roadmap to a new global agreement based on the EU's experience with the Delors Plan of 1984-1985. European experience has underscored that such agreements must address a market need for stability. They cannot result from mere political decisions. The credibility of money represents something that allows more wealth to be available in general. This is linked to market preferences, not only sovereign decisions.

Consequently, the possible roadmap needs to incorporate current trends and start from the awareness of what can be the future if nothing is done, eventually considering if anything can be done or, rather, letting the evolution of the monetary system in the hands of competing and non-cooperative players could even be a better solution.

What would the roadmap look like? In our view, we should start by responding to needs that could arise from the current situation. One necessary but insufficient action would be to reform IMF governance by ensuring greater representation by emerging economies. Such a step would need to be accompanied by a redefinition of the IMF's tools and tasks.

Specifically, the IMF should support stronger cooperation among central banks and help establish a global treaty on the standards for reciprocal acceptance of CBDCs. If the IMF were not the right vehicle for this, consideration should be given to a new monetary institution, supplementary to the IMF, to regulate and ensure the consistency and compatibility of the new digital tools.

This could imply the need for a new agreement which could include "new tools" and eventually commodities that are not only gold in international reserves. Consequently, the first question is whether to enlarge the IMF's scope or to imagine new institutions for new responsibilities. Here the interest of the United States and other Western economies is to reform but not supplant the IMF, the Bank for International Settlements (BIS), the WTO (eventually) and the World Bank Group. Emerging economies might consider other trade-offs.

Any agreed reform is likely to entail a new "protocol of cooperation" among the IMF (and/or other institutions), the WTO and BIS (particularly for payments issues and for the possibility that payment systems "decouple") to ensure consistency and coherence between monetary developments and trade support issues.

This evolution could also be very relevant if central banks need to arrive to an agreement on the role (if commodity or currency-like) of cryptocurrencies (e.g. BitCoins and others) and other hybrid payment mechanisms (e.g. stablecoins) to determine if they should remain as private market tools or be monitored institutionally.

The relevance here is that past monetary systems have always evolved toward holistic and integrated mechanisms that ensured that central banks and governments, retained full public sector control over money and payment systems.

Accepting private money as an alternative to public money in the markets entails acknowledging that markets will stabilize in such a situation. It is difficult to know whether this is a credible and acceptable perspective, or whether the result would be chaos. A debate is needed. Moreover, all main economic players worldwide, not just the West, would need to agree.

If such a debate takes place, optimally in an international forum such as the IMF, the negotiation is likely to lead to the progressive realization of a new Bretton Woods-like agreement, which should either a) mirror the current emerging market trend of a linked multipolar currency scheme (a "quasi-bancor" scenario) anchored to a supranational tool, or b) head towards a new supranational currency anchored to a basket of national currencies bound by soft rules.

The Delors plan for the transition to the euro envisaged a transition through an exchange agreement and a unit of account, the ECU. The goal was to eliminate national currencies without creating a European federal government or a European tax authority. This is still the euro's weakness. The inability of eurozone members to acquire eurozone-level debt means they cannot provide a safe asset in euros able to offset the weight of the U.S. debt in world reserves.

Table 18

Possible phases for a reform of the International Monetary System to be discussed at UN level

- Reform of the current governance of IMF.
- Strengthening of cooperation between central banks establishing a global treaty on the standards for reciprocal acceptance of CBDCs.
- Agreement on which international institution (if IMF or others) should monitor Central Banks reserves and internationally held reserves in non-national currencies. Enlarging the scope for IMF (or other institution) in charge.
- New protocol of cooperation amongst IMF (and/or other institutions), the WTO and BIS (for payments) in order to ensure consistency and coherence amongst monetary developments and trade support issues.
- Agreement on the role (if commodity or currency-like) of cryptocurrencies (eg BitCoin and others) and other hybrid payment mechanism, to determine if those should remain as private market tools or be somehow monitored institutionally.
- Progressive realization of a new "Bretton Woods"-like agreement, which should either mirror the current emerging market trend of a multipolar currency scheme, but somehow linked (a quasi-Bancor scenario) or heading towards a new USD (or equivalent USD/Eur) centred scheme, with other currencies somehow.

The path towards a global currency must of course be compatible with the survival of national currencies, to which it should offer a credible anchor, but under the auspices of an international issuing authority that bears responsibility for its governance. This path can probably be facilitated by technology progress. Especially with the possible spread of CBDCs, technology makes manageable platforms for an efficient use of a global digital currency based on a basket of national CBDCs.

It is certainly a difficult result to achieve, given multiple forces playing conflicting roles in the debate, and given geopolitical pressures. Nevertheless, one thing is likely true: only a new global agreement that recognizes the position of the United States and the West and gives emerging economies a voice commensurate with their weight will ensure continued economic stability geopolitical peace. What can trigger the need for such a discussion and pathway? We acknowledge that in a dollar-centred world, there is little appetite in the United States and other Western economies to do anything that could jeopardize the current system, which has proven to be sustainable, even if suboptimal for non-Western states[158].

Very likely the trigger moment will come when China, as noted above, will be in condition to open up its financial markets fully, gradually making the renminbi fully convertible, allowing the Chinese to freely move capital abroad and allowing foreigners to invest with limited restrictions (comparable to those existing in the West). This would create a more balanced world where the dollar and renminbi might be somehow co-leading stability providers of last resort. It would pressure the United States to manage its public finances and allow Americans to transfer their capital abroad more easily (current anti-money laundering and tax rules are significant burdens to open flows). Likely the world economy would benefit from a more competitive environment.

Is this likely in the short term? No. The full opening of Chinese financial markets would have a completely destabilizing effect today, particularly on the ability of Chinese authorities to retain control over their own economy. This pathway would be possible only on the condition that markets would be free to judge how to allocate resources,[159] including the option for Chinese themselves to freely transfer their capital.

This seems difficult to imagine, given credibility and stability issues and the fact that the possible outcome of a poorly managed "opening" would really be "uncharted territory," including eventual serious geopolitical risks.

On the other hand, if money becomes available with the same basic "rules" globally (so the economy become the common language of all main global sovereign players) this might ensure a long period of peace and prosperity and the rebalancing of global public goods goals. As an obvious consideration, there will be no interest in wars if the common interest of all would be to shift to the economy and everybody will be cross-dependent (and cross-invested) in all the others. In today's geopolitical scenario, this really seems a dream.

The Bretton Woods conference was convened towards the end of the Second World War to define the rules for the world at a time of enormous historical changes. It would be useful to convene a new Bretton Woods-like conference to address the issues of a rapidly evolving world before, not after, a new world war.

Endnotes

1. In this book, Angelo Federico Arcelli is responsible for the chapters 1, 2, 6, 7 and 8 and Giovanni Tria for chapters 3, 4 and 5; introduction and conclusion are shared. The authors also acknowledge Sara Biadetti's contributions in preparing some tables and background research. This book drives from and completes the previous one by Giovanni Tria and Angelo Federico Arcelli, "Towards a new Bretton Woods agreement", Transatlantic Leadership Network, Washington, DC, 2021. The book also incorporates parts previously published by Angelo Federico Arcelli, and notably from Angelo Federico Arcelli's paragraph "the Great illusion" as published in "Dialogue. Open Reflections in a Phase of Transition", 2023, Angelo Federico Arcelli, Agostino Marchetto, Editore Rubbettino, ISBN 9788875744687.), and Angelo Federico Arcelli's article "Moneta e Ricchezza" from the book "Atti della ventesima "Lezione Mario Arcelli" Sostenibilità finanziaria, sostenibilità climatica: il ruolo dei processi decisionali" (editors Daniele Franco and Angelo Federico Arcelli). The first paragraph draws what A. F. Arcelli has been partially published on *Rivista Bancaria*, 2015, I, in A. Privitera, A. F. Arcelli, "An historical perspective to current trends in the banking industry in Europe".

2. Giovanni Tria is honorary professor at the Università di Roma 2–Tor Vergata and a former minister of finance of the Republic of Italy. Angelo Federico Arcelli, PhD, is a full professor (professore straordinario a t.d.) at Università Guglielmo Marconi (Rome), a lecturer at Università Cattolica del Sacro Cuore (Piacenza) and a Senior Fellow of the Center for International Governance Innovation (CIGI, Waterloo, ON, CN).

3. This introduction benefits and takes stock of A.F. Arcelli, "Possible new scenarios for monetary challenges in the years to come" in P.C. Padoan, A.F. Arcelli, eds., "Atti della XIX Lezione Mario Arcelli," Rubbettino editore, 2023 and A.F. Arcelli's contribution to the proceedings of the 2022 Forum Gran Sasso.

4. See A. Privitera and A. F. Arcelli, "An historical perspective to current trends in the banking industry in Europe," in *Rivista Bancaria*, 2015, first quarter.

5. See on this subject the essay by Zhou Xiaochuan, former Governor of the People's Bank of China, "Reform the International Monetary System," Bank for International Settlements, Basel, Switzerland, 2009.

6. We are certainly not talking about a recent debate here. These problems have been on the table for decades. For general background information, see for example Andrew Moravcsik, *The Choice for Europe: Social Purposes and State Power from Messina to Maastricht*, Ithaca, Cornell University Press, 1998; Simon Hix, *What's Wrong with the European Union and How to Fix It*, Cambridge University Press, 2008.

7. See Giovanni Tria, Angelo Federico Arcelli, "Towards a new Bretton Woods agreement," Transatlantic Leadership Network, Washington, DC, 2021.

8. This paragraph draws what A. F. Arcelli has been partially published on *Rivista Bancaria*, 2015, I, in A. Privitera, A. F. Arcelli, "An historical perspective to current trends in the banking industry in Europe". Several parts include contributions (the bulk of the notes and annotations to this paragraph) by research assistant L. Bonamico for adjourning the text.

9. C. P. Kindleberger, "*A Financial History of Western Europe*", Oxford University Press, 1993.

10. L. Einaudi, "From the Franc to the 'Europe': Great Britain, Germany and the attempted transformation of the Latin

Monetary Union into a European Monetary Union," in *Economic History Review* 53 (2), 284–308 (2000).

11. Michael D. Bordo, Robert D. Dittmar and William T. Gavin, "Gold, Fiat, and Price Stability," NBER Working Paper No. 10171, 2003.

12. Kris James Mitchener, Masato Shizume and Marc D. Weidenmier, "Why Did Countries Adopt the Gold Standard? Lessons from Japan," NBER Working Paper No. 15195, 2009.

13. Craig K. Elwell, Brief History of the Gold Standard in the United States, Congressional Research Service, 2011.

14. Richard N. Cooper, "The Gold Standard: Historical Facts and Future Prospects," Brookings Papers on Economic Activity, 1982.

15. W. F. V. Vanthoor, "*European Monetary Union Since 1848: a Political and Historical Analysis*", Cheltenham, 1996; also, see M. Flandreu, "On the Inflationary Bias of Common Currencies: The Latin Union Puzzle," European Economic Review, North-Holland, 1993.

16. Henry Parker Willis, "A History of The Latin Monetary Union: A Study of International Monetary Action", The University of Chicago Press, Chicago, 1901.

17. A. Redish, "The Latin Monetary Union and the emergence of the international gold standard," in M. Bordo and F. Capie, *Monetary Regimes in Transition* (Studies in Macroeconomic History), Cambridge University Press, Cambridge, 1993.

18. Macdonald, James, "A Free Nation Deep in Debt," (https://2think.org/debt.shtml#:~:text=But%20in%20the%20eighteenth%20century%20it%20was%20commonly,with%20some%20fundamental%20questions%3A%20Why%20do%20governments%20borrow%3).

19. M. Flandreau, "Was the Latin Monetary Union a Franc Zone?" in Reis J. (ed.), *International Monetary Systems in*

Historical Perspective, Palgrave Macmillan, London, 1995. The Union included France, Spain, Italy, Belgium, Switzerland, Papal States and several other states over time.

20. Kee-Hong Bae, Warren Bailey, "The Latin Monetary Union: Some evidence on Europe's failed common currency," *Review of Development Finance*, p. 131-149, 2011. Although the Latin Monetary Union existed on paper until 1927, it effectively ended with the outbreak of World War I in June 1914. In that occasion, the Latin Monetary Union members suspended the open conversion of money to gold, effectively ending what was left of the union.

21. L. Einaudi, "From the Franc to the 'Europe': Great Britain, Germany and the attempted transformation of the Latin Monetary Union into a European Monetary Union," *Economic History Review* 53 (2), 284–308 (2000).

22. Kenneth Moure "The Gold Standard Illusion: France, the Bank of France, and the International Gold Standard, 1914-1939", Oxford University Press, 2002.

23. Ben S. Bernanke, "The World on a Cross of Gold: A Review of "Golden Fetters": The Gold Standard and the Great Depression, 1919–1939," *Journal of Monetary Economics*, 1993.

24. Michael D. Bordo, Antu P. Murshid, "The International Transmission of Financial Crises before World War II: Was there Contagion?", Rutgers University, 1999. And Barry Eichengreen and Marc Flandreu, "*The Gold Standard in Theory and History*", Routledge, London, 1993.

25. Paul R. Krugman, Maurice Obstfeld, Marc J. Melitz "*International Economics, Theory and Policy*", Pearson, United Kingdom, Chapter 19, pp. 579–598, 2018.

26. Niall Ferguson (2001). The Cash Nexus: Money and Power in the Modern World 1700-2000, Basic Books, New York.

27. Michael D. Bordo, "The Gold Standard, Bretton Woods and other Monetary Regimes: An Historical Appraisal," NBER Working Paper No. 4310, 1993.

28. Elaboration by Sara Biadetti on the Maddison Project database 2023. See MPD version 2023: Bolt, Jutta and Jan Luiten van Zanden, "Maddison style estimates of the evolution of the world economy: A new 2023 update", Journal of Economic Surveys, 1–41, 2024.

29. Michael D. Bordo, Antu P. Murshid, "The International Transmission of Financial Crises before World War II: Was there Contagion?" –Rutgers University, 1999.

30. John Maynard Keynes, "Proposals for an International Clearing Union," 1943, in Keith Horsefield et al., *The International Monetary Fund 1945-1965: Twenty Years of International Monetary Cooperation*, Volume 1. Chronicle, International Monetary Fund, Washington DC, 1966.

31. Elaboration by Sara Biadetti on the Maddison Project database 2023. See MPD version 2023: Bolt, Jutta and Jan Luiten van Zanden, "Maddison style estimates of the evolution of the world economy: A new 2023 update", Journal of Economic Surveys, 1–41, 2024.

32. Elaboration on IMF and IFS data by Sara Biadetti. Note: one troy ounce corresponds to 31,1034768 grams.

33. R. J. Bartel "International Monetary Unions: The Nineteenth Century Experience", *The Journal of European Economic History*, 1974. Also, see Pollard, S., "The Integration of the European Economy since 1815," *Economic History*, 1981.

34. Elaboration on ECB data by Sara Biadetti.

35. Niccolò Battistini, Marco Pagano, Saverio Simonelli, "Systemic Risk, Sovereign Yields and Bank Exposures in the Euro Crisis," *Economic Policy*, Vol. 29, Issue 78, 2014.

36. Fred Bergsten, "The Dollar and the Euro," *Foreign Affairs 76*, 2004.

37. Patricia S. Pollard, "The Creation of the Euro and the Role of the Dollar in International Markets," The Federal Reserve Bank of St. Louis, 2001.

38. Erin Blakemore, "The Euro: How a Common Currency Helped Europe Achieve Peace," History Stories, 2018.

39. Jacopo Cimadomo, Sebastian Hauptmeier, Alessandra Anna Palazzo and Alexander Popov, "Risk Sharing in the Euro Area", *ECB Economic Bulletin*, Issue 3, 2018.

40. Source: https://www.weforum.org/agenda/2015/03/what-caused-the-big-spreads-on-eurozone-bonds/. WEF site refers that "*After the introduction of the euro, the interest rates on government debt in the EMU member countries converged to low levels that were previously reserved for the sovereign bonds of core AAA-rated countries, such as Germany. The borrowing costs of the peripheral countries not only decreased, but also became insensitive to fiscal fundamentals in respective countries*". And "*The period of homogenous and low sovereign interest rates ended with the onset of the Greek crisis and the discussions concerning a Eurozone bail-out of Greece. The Greek crisis constitutes a turning point in the pricing of sovereign bonds in the Eurozone, as markets started to demand high premia for default risk.*". So that "*The convergence of interest rates within the Eurozone and the re-emergence of spreads at the time of the Greek crisis constitutes a new puzzle in international macroeconomics.*".

41. This part has been partially published in *Rivista Bancaria*, 2015, I, in A. Privitera, A. F. Arcelli, "An historical perspective to current trends in the banking industry in Europe." This revision benefits from added insights from L. Bonamico.

42. Benoit Coeuré: "Should the ECB Care About the Euro's Global Role?", Voxeu CEPR, 2019.

43. Andrea Boltho and Wendy Carlin: "The Problems of European Monetary Union—Asymmetric Shocks or Asymmetric Behavior," Voxeu CEPR, 2012.

44. Alberto Alesina, Daron Acemoglu and Christopher J. Bickerton, "The Search for Europe: Contrasting Approaches," BBVA, 2016.

45. Andrew Moravcsik "The Choice for Europe: Social Purposes and State Power from Messina to Maastricht" Ithaca: Cornell University Press, 2018. Also: Simon Hix, "What's Wrong with the European Union and How to Fix It", Cambridge, Polity, 2008.

46. Peter A. Hall, "Varieties of Capitalism and the Euro Crisis," *West European Politics* 37, 2014.

47. European Central Bank (2019). "The International Role of the Euro." Also see Barry Eichengreen, "The Breakup of the Euro Area," NBER Working Paper No. 13393, 2007.

48. M. Mitsopoulos and T. Pelagidis, "*Understanding the Crisis in Greece*", Houndmills: Palgrave Macmillan, 2012. Also see Peter A. Hall, "The Euro Crisis and the Future of European Integration," BBVA, Madrid, 2016.

49. Michael D. Bordo and Lars Jonung, "The Future of the EMU: What Does the History of Monetary Union Tell Us?" NBER Working Paper No. 7365, 1999.

50. Matthias Matthijs and Mark Blyth, "*The Future of the Euro*", Oxford University Press, 2015.

51. Martin Feldstein, "The Political Economy of the European Economic and Monetary Union: Political Sources of an Economic Liability," NBER Working Paper No. 6150, 1998.

52. The Covid-19 crisis once again changed the landscape and casts new shadows on the future, and although it is still unclear the real path that European Union will follow in the coming decades and, notably, if it will be leaning towards a

"single market of sovereign states" or at least a partial political union. From today's perspective, the latter seems unlikely.

53. See J. Rueff, The Monetary Sin of the West, pag. 78, The Macmillan Company, 866 Third Avenue, New York, N.Y. 10022 Collier-Macmillan Canada Ltd., Toronto, Ontario - The Monetary Sin of the West was originally published in French by Librairie Plon under the title Le Péché Monêtaìre de l'Occident and is reprinted by permission. Library of Congress Catalog Card Number: 79-182450, Second Printing, 1972.

54. Elaboration by Sara Biadetti. Source: World Bank national accounts data, and OECD National Accounts data files. between 1970 and 1988 trade data on BRICS exclude Imports and Exports for Brazil and Russian Federation.

55. Robert Triffin, "Gold and the Dollar Crisis", New Haven: Yale University Press, 1960.

56. Ferguson N., "The Cash Nexus: Money and Power in the Modern World 1700–2000", Basic Books, New York, 2001.

57. Peter M. Garber, "The Collapse of the Bretton Woods Fixed Exchange Rate System," in A Retrospective on the Bretton Woods System: Lesson for International Monetary Reform, University of Chicago Press, 1993.

58. Ethan Ilzetzki, Carmen M. Reinhart and Kenneth S. Rogoff "Why is the Euro Punching Below its Weight?", NBER Working Paper No. 26760, 2020.

59. Peter Kugler, "The Bretton Woods System: Design and Operation, in Money in the Western Legal Tradition", Oxford University Press, Oxford, 2016.

60. Elaboration by Sara Biadetti on the Maddison Project database 2023. See MPD version 2023: Bolt, Jutta and Jan Luiten van Zanden, "Maddison style estimates of the evolution of

the world economy: A new 2023 update", Journal of Economic Surveys, 1–41, 2024.

61. Weizhen Tan, "The Growing U.S. Deficit Raises Questions About Funding as China Cuts U.S. Debt Holdings," CNBC, 2020.

62. Zhou Xiaochuan "Reform the International Monetary System," Bank for International Settlements, Basel, Switzerland, 2009.

63. See also Ito, H., and R. McCauley, "Currency Composition of Foreign Exchange Reserves". Journal of International Money and Finance, Volume 102 (April 2020, 102-104) and Chinn, M, H Ito, and Robert N McCauley, "Do Central Banks Rebalance Their Currency Shares?". NBER Working Paper No. w29190 (August 2021).

64. Elaboration by Sara Biadetti on the Maddison Project database 2023. See MPD version 2023: Bolt, Jutta and Jan Luiten van Zanden, "Maddison style estimates of the evolution of the world economy: A new 2023 update", Journal of Economic Surveys, 1–41, 2024.

65. Samantha Pearson & Aloisio Alves, "Brazil says a word in a "Currency War," Reuters, 2010.

66. UNCTAD data (https://unric.org/it/commercio-globale-me-no-5-per-cento-unctad/) suggest that Global trade for 2023 is around 30.7 trillion U.S. Dollars, around 1.5 trillion lower than in 2022.

67. Elaboration by Sara Biadetti on World Bank data. U.S. data missing for 2023.

68. Elaboration on IMF data by Sara Biadetti.

69. For a debate on this issue, see Ilzetzki E., Reinhart C.M., Rogoff K.S., "Rethinking Exchange Rate Regimes", 2021. Draft prepared for Gita Gopinath, Elhanan Helpman and Kenneth Rogoff, eds., Handbook of International Economics vol.5, and Serkan A., Eichengreen B. and Simpson-Bell C., "The stealth

erosion of dollar dominance and the rise of nontraditional reserve currencies," *Journal of International Economics*, 2022.

70. Elaboration on data from Banca d'Italia by Sara Biadetti.

71. See Ilzetzki E., Reinhart C.M., Rogoff K.S., "Rethinking Exchange Rate Regimes", 2021.

72. See Goodhart and Pradhan, "The Great Demographic Reversal," 2020.

73. Elaboration on data from Banca d'Italia by Sara Biadetti.

74. See: Ilzetzki E., Reinhart C.M., Rogoff K.S., "Rethinking Exchange Rate Regimes", 2021.

75. Elaboration on IMF data by Sara Biadetti.

76. See Goodhart and Pradhan, op. cit.

77. Elaboration on data from Banca d'Italia by Sara Biadetti.

78. From: Historical Parallels to Today's Inflationary Episode | CEA | The White House – figure 1.

79. See Cofer and IMF Reserve data template.

80. See Serkan Arslanalp, Barry Eichengreen, Chima Simpson-Bell, 2022, *Journal of International Economics*.

81. See Serkan Arslanalp, Barry Eichengreen, Chima Simpson-Bell, 2022, *Journal of International Economics*.

82. See Goodhart and Pradan, 2020, cit.

83. This text reproduces and elaborates on the speech "Global public goods and industrial policy" by Giovanni Tria at the Beijing Forum "The Harmony of Civilizations and Prosperity for All" Beijing November 4th, 2023.

84. See BIS "Central banks and payments in the digital era", Glossary to the Annual Economic Report, Chapter III, Basel, 2020.

85. See Bech, Morten L. and Garratt, Rodney: "Central Bank Cryptocurrencies", BIS Quarterly Review, September 2017.

86. See Oliver Wyman Forum, AWS: "Retail Central Bank, Digital Currency: From Vision to Design—A framework to align policy objectives and technology design choices", March 2022, page 9.

87. This part is reproposing the part of A.F. Arcelli of the article "IMF Special Drawing Rights allocation as a first step towards a new economic order", by A.F. Arcelli and A. Privitera, ISEA Centro Studi, 2022.

88. See: https://www.imf.org/en/Topics/special-drawing-right.

89. See: https://www.imf.org/external/pubs/ft/aa/index.htm – for the entire downloadable official text. "The Articles of Agreement of the International Monetary Fund were adopted at the United Nations Monetary and Financial Conference (Bretton Woods, New Hampshire) on July 22, 1944. They were originally accepted by 29 countries and since then have been signed and ratified by a total of 190 Member countries. As the charter of the organization, the Articles lay out the Fund's purposes, which include the promotion of 'international monetary cooperation through a permanent institution which provides the machinery for consultation and collaboration on international monetary problems'. The Articles also establish the mandate of the Organization and its members' rights and obligations, its governance structure, and roles of its organs, and lays out various rules of operations including those relating to the conduct of its operations and transactions regarding the Special Drawing Rights. The key functions of the IMF are the surveillance of the international monetary system and the monitoring of members' economic and financial policies, the provision of Fund resources to member countries in need, and the delivery of technical assistance and financial services. Since their adoption in 1944, the Articles of Agreement have been amended seven times, with the latest

amendment adopted on December 15, 2010 (effective January 26, 2016). The Articles are complemented by the By-laws of the Fund adopted by the Board of Governors, themselves being supplemented by the Rules and Regulations adopted by the Executive Board.".

90. See, inter alia, Vreeland, James Raymond, "The IMF and economic development", Cambridge University Press, 2003; and Wilkie, Christopher, "Special drawing rights (SDRs): The first international money", Oxford University Press, 2012. (2004): 1–25. Press, 2007; and Despres, Emil, Charles Kindleberger, and William Salant. 1966, "The Dollar and World liquidity: A minority view". Economist (February) :526–29; and De Vries, Margaret Garritsen, "The IMF in a changing world, 1945–85", Washington, DC: International Monetary Fund, 1986; and Diz, Adolfo C. 1984, "The conditions attached to adjustment financing: Evolution of the IMF practice". In "The International Monetary System: Forty Years after Bretton Woods", 214–325. Conference Series no. 28. Federal Reserve Bank of Boston, May. Dornbusch, Rudiger. 1976, 'Expectations and exchange rate dynamics', Journal of Political Economy 84: 1161–76; and Ocampo, José Antonio, 13, 'Special Drawing Rights and the Reform of the Global Reserve System in Reforming the International Financial System for Development', pp. 314-342. Columbia University Press, 2011; and Eichengreen, Barry and Jeffrey Sachs (2009), "Exchange Rates and Economic Recovery in the 1930s", Cambridge University Press.

91. See: https://www.imf.org/en/About/FactsheetsSheets/2016/08/01/14/51/Special-Drawing-Right-SDR. Note that: "The Articles of Agreement, determine that under certain conditions, the IMF may allocate SDRs to members participating in the SDR Department (currently all members of the IMF). A general allocation of SDRs must be consistent with the objective of meeting the long-term global need to supplement existing reserve assets and receive broad support from the IMF's membership (an allocation requires Board of Governors ap-

proval by an 85 percent majority of the total voting power of the members in the SDR Department). Once agreed, the allocation is distributed to member countries in proportion to their quota shares at the Fund. A special one-time allocation in 2009 enabled countries that joined the IMF after 1981 (e.g. after previous allocations) to participate in the SDR system on an equitable basis."

92. The 15 "prescribed holders" allowed to hold SDRs are the European Central Bank (ECB), the Bank of Central African States, the Central Bank of West African States, and the Eastern Caribbean Central Bank; the BIS, the Arab Monetary Fund, the Latin American Reserve Fund and eight development institutions: the African Development Bank, the African Development Fund, the Asian Development Bank, the International Bank for Reconstruction and Development and the International Development Association, the Islamic Development Bank, Nordic Investment Bank, and the International Fund for Agricultural Development.

93. See: https://www.imf.org/enAbout/Factsheets/Sheets/2016/08/01/14/51/Special-Drawing-Right-SDR. In particular: "Participating members and prescribed holders can buy and sell SDRs in the voluntary market. If required, the IMF can also designate members to buy SDRs from other participants. SDRs may be used by IMF members and the IMF itself in accordance with the Articles of Agreement and decisions adopted by the Executive Board and Board of Governors. The IMF has the authority to prescribe other holders of SDRs, non-members, member countries that are not SDR Department Participants, institutions that perform the functions of a central bank for more than one member, and other official entities. As of end-January 2021, there were 15 organizations approved as prescribed holders. Prescribed holders may not receive allocations of SDRs. SDRs cannot be held by private entities or individuals".

94. See also: https://www.imf.org/en/About/Factsheets/Sheets/
2016/08/01/14/51/Special-Drawing-Right-SDR—The weights
determined in the 2015 Review (to be amended as of 2022)
define the fixed number of units of currency for a 5-year period starting Oct 1, 2016 as follows: the U.S. dollar at 0.58252,
the euro at 0.38671, the Chinese yuan at 1.0174, the Japanese
yen at 11.900 and the pound sterling at 0.085946. The SDR
value in terms of the U.S. dollar is determined daily based on
the spot exchange rates observed at around noon London
time and posted on the IMF website. It should be noted that
"currencies included in the SDR basket have to meet two criteria: the export criterion and the freely usable criterion. A currency meets the export criterion if its issuer is an IMF member or a monetary union that includes IMF members and is
also one of the top five world exporters. For a currency to be
determined "freely usable" by the IMF, it must be widely used
to make payments for international transactions and widely
traded in the principal exchange markets. Freely usable currencies can be used in Fund financial transactions". The SDR
is not a currency but can be used as a unit of account. In fact,
"the SDR serves as the unit of account of the IMF and some
other international organizations". It is important to recall that
SDRs' value "is determined weekly based on a weighted average of representative interest rates on short-term government
debt instruments in the money markets of the SDR basket
currencies, with a floor of 5 basis points. It is posted on the
IMF website". It "provides the basis for calculating the interest
rate charged to members on their non-concessional borrowing from the IMF and paid to members for their remunerated
creditor positions in the IMF. It is also the interest paid to
members on their SDR holdings and charged on their SDR
allocation".

95. See Boughton, James M., "From Suez to Tequila: The IMF
as Crisis Manager", Economic Journal, Vol. 110 (January), pp.
273–91, and Boughton, James M. 2001a, 'Silent Revolution:

The International Monetary Fund 1979–1989' (Washington: International Monetary Fund).

96. Ekpenyong, David B, "Can the special drawing right (SDR) become an acceptable reserve currency of the international monetary fund (IMF) in the midst of strong resistance by developed countries captained by the USA?", Journal of Financial Management & Analysis 20, no. 1 (2007).

97. See Harrison, Matthew, and Geng Xiao, "China and Special Drawing Rights—Towards a Better International Monetary System". Journal of Risk and Financial Management 12, no. 2 (2019): 60 and Helleiner, Eric, and Bessma Momani, "The hidden history of China and the IMF. The great wall of money: Power and politics in China's international monetary relations (2014)", 45–70.

98. See Alessandrini, Pietro. "Il Bancor". Working Paper No. 84. Money and Finance Research group (Mo. Fi. R.), Univ. Politecnica Marche-Dept. Economic and Social Sciences, 2013.

99. See Wilkie, Christopher, "Special drawing rights (SDRs): The first international money", Oxford University Press, 2012. (2004): 1–25. Press, 2007. See also Wang, Hongying, "China and the International Monetary System: Does Beijing Really Want to Challenge the Dollar?", Foreign Affairs, SNAPSHOT, December 19th, 2017.

100. See Emminger, Otmar, "Practical aspects of the problem of balance of payments adjustment", Journal of Political Economy 75 (August 1967),12–22. See also Bordo, Michael D., and Anna J. Schwartz , "Transmission of real and monetary disturbances under fixed and floating rates. In Dollars, Dejkits and Trade", ed. James A. Dorn and William A. Niskanen, 237–58. Boston: Kluwer Academic, 1989.

101. International Monetary Fund. 2018b, "Considerations on the Role of the SDR", Policy Paper, April 11, 2018. See also

Kenen, Peter, "An SDR-based Reserve System", Journal of Globalization and Development, 2010b.

102. See: https://www.imf.org/enNews/Articles/2021/07/08/pr 21208-imf-managing-director-kristalina-georgieva-executive-board-backing-new-us650b-sdr-allocation.

103. See. https://www.imf.org/en/About/FAQ/special-drawing-right

104. See Camdessus, Michel "An agenda for the IMF at the start of the 21st Century", Remarks at the Council on Foreign Relations, February, New York, 2010.

105. See Alessandrini, Pietro, and Michele U. Fratianni, 'International Monies, Special Drawing Rights, and Supernational Money', Special Drawing Rights, and Supernational Money (July 3, 2009).

106. See K. Georgeva speech, Singapore Fintech Festival, 15 November 2023.

107. This part extensively draw on Angelo Federico Arcelli's paragraph "The great illusion" from the book "Dialogue", by His eminence cardinal Agostino Marchetto and Angelo Federico Arcelli, Soveria Mannelli (CZ, Italy, 2023) and also takes stock of the work recently published by A.F. Arcelli ("Possible new scenarios for monetary challenges in the years to come") in P.C. Padoan, A.F. Arcelli, "Atti della XIX Lezione Mario Arcelli", Rubbettino editore, 2023 and, by A.F. Arcelli, in the proceeds for 2022 Forum Gran Sasso meetings.

108. Michael D. Bordo, Robert D. Dittmar and William T. Gavin (2003). "Gold, Fiat, and Price Stability," NBER Working Paper No. 10171.

109. John Maynard Keynes, "Proposals for an International Clearing Union," in Keith Horsefield et al., The International Monetary Fund 1945–1965: Twenty Years of International Monetary Cooperation, Volume 1. Chronicle, International Monetary Fund, Washington DC, 1966.

110. For some historical references, and with no claim to impor-
tance or exhaustiveness, here are some interesting texts on the
concepts proposed, see for example Charles P. Kindleberger, *A
Financial History of Western Europe*, Oxford University Press,
Oxford (UK), 1993; and M. Flandreau 'Was the Latin Monetary
Union a Franc Zone?' in Reis J. (ed.), *International Monetary
Systems in Historical Perspective*, Palgrave Macmillan, London
(UK), 1995; and also Kenneth Moure, *The Gold Standard
Illusion: France, the Bank of France, and the International Gold
Standard, 1914–1939*, Oxford University Press, Oxford (UK),
2002; or L. Einaudi (2000), 'From the Franc to the 'Europe':
Great Britain, Germany and the attempted transformation of
the Latin Monetary Union into a European Monetary Union',
Economic History Review, 53 (2), 284–308, 2000.

111. For background information, see for example Ben S. Bernanke,
'The World on a Cross of Gold: A Review of "Golden Fetters":
The Gold Standard and the Great Depression, 1919–1939', in
Journal of Monetary Economics, I, 1993; and Craig K. Elwell,
'Brief History of the Gold Standard in the United States',
Congressional Research Service, Washington, DC (USA),
2011; and also Richard N. Cooper 'The Gold Standard:
Historical Facts and Future Prospects' in *Brookings Papers on
Economic Activity*, Washington, DC (USA), 1982.

112. In this case we talk about the "market failures". Of course, stat-
ing this might contradict the well-known positions of Adam
Smith in "*The wealth of the nations (An inquiry into the nature
and causes of the wealth of the nations*", March 1776) and the
conviction that an "invisible hand", given by the smooth functioning of the free market always produces optimal results.
Nevertheless, this is a thesis that has probably been widely
discussed by economists, including in the past, to the point
that as early as the 19th Century, Vilfredo Pareto (1848–1923)
had advanced the idea of "relative" economic optimalities
(which would later be defined as "Pareto optimalities") to
show that (forgive the extreme simplification), under certain

conditions, the market does not always find the best solution. Since this is a well-known debate and somewhat removed from the subjects dealt with here, I shall allow the reader to form their own ideas.

113. See for example the publications of Benoit Coeuré, a member of the Executive Board of the ECB, "Should the ECB Care About the Euro's Global Role?", Voxeu, CEPR, 2019; the European Central Bank, "The International Role of the Euro", Frankfurt (D), 2019; and Barry Eichengreen, "The Breakup of the Euro Area", NBER Working Paper No. 13393, 2007.

114. See also John Maynard Keynes, *The Collected Writings*, Vol. 26, Activities, "1941–46: Shaping the Post-War World: Bretton Woods and Reparations", London, (UK), Macmillan, reprinted 1980. An analysis of the impacts of the reparations imposed at the end of the First World War and of the potential implications of creating an unbalanced monetary system at the end of the Second World War shows how the smooth functioning of the monetary system and of the trade system is interdependent. Any asymmetry could have serious consequences (as history has since demonstrated).

115. We need here to consider that all the above does not completely apply when a country decides not to have a convertible currency, albeit it could have it. This is the case for China, which does not allow for the renminbi to be convertible and does not allow for financial flows (private ones) to be freely possible from and to China. Clearly there are several good reasons, also to maintain stability, for such choices. But let's not forget what all this means for the World.

116. Hardly any of the bank crises of the last few years have been caused by queues of account holders at the counters; they happened because the regulators (above all central banks and governments) established the ceasing of activity and the resolution (or aggregation, or another hypothesis) of the bank in crisis before it collapsed. This is often justified by the need to

preserve the stability of the system, but it is also the clearest confirmation of the importance of market confidence, in both the regulator and the system and in every single regulated banking and financial institution.

117. For background information, see James Buchanan, *"John Law: A Scottish Adventurer of the Eighteenth Century"*, MacLehose Press, 2018.

118. See also Barry Eichengreen, "The Gold Standard and the Great Depression, 1919–1939", Oxford University Press, Oxford, 1992 and Michael D. Bordo with Barry Eichengreen, "The Rise and Fall of a Barbarous Relic: The Role of Gold in the International Monetary System", University of Chicago Press, Chicago (IL), USA, 1998.

119. Somehow all this impacts all World currencies, implying that the monetary area represented by China has relatively few say on Global monetary policies if compared to the U.S. On the other hand, it would likely seem that all Western economies need to preserve the relative credibility of the Western currencies to preserve their own wealth. Any new Bretton Woods would need to come from a shared compromise and not from unilateral appetites, which very likely would not lead to any conclusive agreement.

120. See Henry M. Paulson Jr., "The Future of the Dollar" in *Foreign Affairs (USA)*, 19 May 2020. According to Paulson, who was the U.S. Secretary of the Treasury at that time, the USA didn't seek out the exorbitant privilege; it was a consequence of the scheme resulting from the Bretton Woods negotiations and from the events of the following decades.

121. In this regard, see Graham K. Shaw's *"Aspettative razionali. Una esposizione elementare"*, ISDN 9788813168780, translated by M.G. Legrenzi and published by CEDAM, Padua, 1990.

122. These ideas had already been set out in 1987 by George Soros, the famous financier, in his book *"The Alchemy of Finance –*

reading the mind of the markets", published by John Wiley and Sons, London (UK), 1987. As we all remember, his name was not known to the public until the events of September 1992, when the positions taken by his "hedge funds" led to a crisis in the European monetary system and the rapid exit of the Italian lira and the British pound from the system. Soros had gambled on the market believing that the authorities of those two countries could not "defend" the official parities of their currencies, which were unsustainable in their economic fundamentals. Despite the efforts of the two central banks and the statements of governors with historic stature, such as the Italian Carlo A. Ciampi, the markets caused the defeat of the authorities in the space of a few days. It was perhaps the first case in history, or at least the first one of such significance, in which a series of initiatives by private speculative operators succeeded in forcing the public authorities and governments of Western countries to abandon an economic policy line that had been officially declared and was backed by concrete actions. For the first time it was clear that the "credibility" of even the most significant institutions had its limits.

123. Here, too, see Graham K. Shaw's book *Aspettative razionali.* ..., cit.

124. Cryptocurrencies, such as BitCoin, Ethereum and the like, are not "money", legally speaking, given that they are not issued by a central bank and have no legal value.

125. The acronym CBDCs stands for Central Bank Digital Currencies. They are nothing more than different forms of existing currencies (a dollar or a euro remain the same, it's just that – and it is not yet entirely clear in what sphere – they would acquire new functions and become purely digital currencies).

126. G. Gopinath, Chief Economist at the International Monetary Fund, makes some interesting considerations in his article entitled 2Digital currencies will not displace the dominant dollar", published in the *Financial Times* on 7 January 2020.

127. This has been proven not only by the digital currency bubble in recent years, but also by the search for new, non-banking ways to regulate their financial commitments, in a trend that seems to have been exacerbated rather than reduced by geopolitical tension, such as that which exploded in 2022–23.

128. See Oliver Wyman Forum, AWS, "Retail Central Bank, Digital Currency: From Vision to Design—A framework to align policy objectives and technology design choices", March 2022, page 9.

129. It is always interesting to recall Keynes on the role of IMF ("Proposals for an International Clearing Union", in Keith Horsefield et al, *"The International Monetary Fund 1945–1965: Twenty Years of International Monetary Cooperation"*, Volume 1, Chronicle, International Monetary Fund, Washington DC., 1965.

130. Today, we really do not yet see any that can bring about a revolution in the system, but we cannot rule it out for tomorrow.

131. See John Maynard Keynes, *"The Collected Writings"*, Vol. 26, Activities, 1941–46: 'Shaping the Post-War World: Bretton Woods and Reparations', London (UK), Macmillan ed., reprinted 1980.

132. To go back to the example already cited, it is very likely that someone who lives in an emerging country will prefer to hold or buy an asset in a country that they perceive as more stable (with a "stronger" currency) to safeguard their capital. As a form of aggregate behavior, this will produce an ever-widening gap between the two countries, and it will worsen the situation of the "weaker" currency to the advantage of the "stronger" one.

133. See Masera R., "Old and New Risks: Challenges Ahead", Enel Risk Academy, Rome, November 9th, 2021.

134. In practice, this will mean that the citizen of the "weak" country will not necessarily want to hold assets in the "strong"

country anymore because they will be able to safeguard their capital by holding "new bancors". In the end, the gap in the value of assets in the two areas will probably narrow (subject to the other causes of difference, of course) and this will reduce the wealth of the "strong" countries and perhaps increase that of the "weak" countries.

135. See Arcelli A., Masera R. and Tria G., "Da Versailles a Bretton Woods: errori storici e modelli ancora attuali per un sistema monetario internazionale sostenibile", in *Moneta e Credito*, Rome, December 2021.

136. See Michael D. Bordo "The Bretton Woods International Monetary System: A Historical Overview", in *A retrospective on the Bretton Woods System: Lessons for International Monetary Reform* by Michael D. Bordo and Barry Eichengreen, University of Chicago Press, Chicago (IL), USA, 1993.

137. As a reference, see the theories of Patricia S. Pollard in "The Creation of the Euro and the role of the Dollar in International Markets", The Federal Reserve Bank of St. Louis Working Papers, USA, 2001.

138. See also A. Greenspan, "Hearing, House Oversight Committee", U.S. Congress, Proceedings, 23 October 2008.

139. See Henry Farrell and Abraham L. Newman, "Weaponized Interdependence. How Global Economic Networks Shape State Coercion", *International Security*, Vol. 44, No. 1., 2019.

140. See A. F. Arcelli and G. Tria, "Time to reset?", in *World Commerce Review*, Q2 2021, available at: https://www.world-commercereview.com/publications/article_pdf/1966 .

141. See J. B. Rawls, "*A Theory of Justice*", originally published in 1971, reprinted as "*Una teoria della giustizia*", Feltrinelli, Milan, 2008.

142. See J.K. Galbraith, "*The Affluent Society*" (originally published in 1958), translated into Italian by Giorgio Badiali and Sergio Cotta with the title *Economia e benessere*, published by

Comunità, Milan, 1959; and then as *La società opulenta*, ivi, 19632; Boringhieri, Turin, 1969.

143. This chapter extensively draw on Angelo Federico Arcelli's paragraph "How can we find a way out of this uncertainty" from the book "Dialogue", by His eminence cardinal Agostino Marchetto and Angelo Federico Arcelli, Soveria Mannelli (CZ), Italy, 2023.

144. See A.F. Arcelli and G. Tria, "Towards a Renewed Bretton Woods", Washington D.C., Transatlantic Leadership Network, January 2021.

145. See J.M. Keynes, *The Economic Consequences of the Peace*, New York: Harcourt, Brace and Howe, 1920.

146. See B. Bernanke, "The Macro Economics of the Great Depression: A Comparative Approach", Journal of Money, Credit and Banking, 27 (1), 1995, pp. 1–28.

147. See J.E. Stiglitz. *"The Euro: How a Common Currency Threatens the Future of Europe"*, W. W. Norton & Company, New York, 2016.

148. See also M.D. Bordo and P.L. Siklos, "Central Bank Credibility: An Historical and Quantitative Exploration, in Central Bank at a Crossroads", Cambridge University Press, Cambridge, (UK), 2016.

149. See M. Draghi (2016), "Addressing the causes of low interest rates", introductory speech by the ECB President at the Annual Meeting of the Asian Development Bank, Frankfurt am Main, 2 May, available at: https://www.ecb.europa.eu/press/key/date/2016/html/sp160502.en.html

150. See A.F Arcelli, C. Gorino C. and C. Torcellan, "Le prospettive del credito in Italia, dopo la crisi pandemica e l'attesa fine del temporary framework", Minerva Bancaria, 4–5/2021, pp. 155–175.

151. See A.F. Arcelli, R.S. Masera and G. Tria, "Da Versailles a Bretton Woods e ai giorni nostri: errori storici e modelli anco-

ra attuali per un sistema monetario internazionale sostenibile", *Moneta e Credito*, Rome, 2022.

152. See A.F Arcelli, C. Gorino C. and C. Torcellan, "La situazione del Mercato del credito in Italia dopo la pandemia e in vista della fine del "Temporary Framework" europeo", Quaderni DISES, no. 152/September, Piacenza: Dipartimento di Scienze Economiche e Sociali, Università Cattolica del Sacro Cuore, available at: https://dipartimenti.unicatt.it/dises-Arcelli-Gorino-Torcellan_152.pdf.

153. Some reflections that are always valid can be found in the paper by Alberto Alesina, Silvia Ardagna and Vincenzo Galasso, "The Euro and Structural Reforms", NBER – National Bureau of Economic Research, Boston (MA), USA, Working Paper No. 14479, 2008.

154. It also seemed to have created an implicit constraint towards a long-term goal of political union, in part given the near impossibility for any member country to leave the Union without causing collapsing its own economy to collapse.

155. Henry Farrell and Abraham L. Newman, "Weaponized Interdependence. How Global Economic Networks Shape State Coercion," International Security, Vol. 44, No. 1 (2019).

156. "Derisking" has led to conflicting behaviors. On the one hand, Western policies are being advanced in part to improve air quality and reduce car pollution. On the other hand, given that China has become the global leader in producing power batteries for cars, the United States and then the EU levied import taxes on Chinese products to support national producers, and for strategic reasons, even though Chinese products cannot be substituted quickly by local production. The result: Western countries will likely slow down their efforts to meet their clean air objectives to ensure higher levels of industrial independence. Our thesis is that trade, economic and monetary cooperation are required to produce and sustain global common goods. Clearly, this is not something to do at any

cost; the United States and other Western countries must align their goals with their interest in preserving and even enhancing their position. Since the West's wealth is linked to the value of its currencies, the goal is to protect and preserve the role of the U.S. dollar and the Euro.

157. The Economic and Monetary Union (EMU) was established by a decision of the European Council on June 1988 and commissioned by the EU Commission President, Jacques Delors, to draw up a program. This "Delors committee" was composed by the governors of the national central banks of the European Community, Alexandre Lamfalussy, then Director-General of the Bank for International Settlements, Niels Thygesen and Miguel Boyer, in those years respectively Professor of Economics in Denmark and Chairman of the Banco Exterior de España. The "Delors Report", drawn up at the end of the work, proposed to articulate the realization of economic and monetary union in three distinct phases.

158. The only pressure that might push Western countries to go down this road is what history teaches us: if in the 18th century the French aristocracy would have anticipated where their heads would have ben at stake, we would likely live today in a very different world. Let's not forget that the aristocracy, now, is the West

159. History also teaches us what happens when the superstructures of governance are imposed on a reality which goes on different paths. The end of the Soviet Union should be studied with a backward-looking and a forward-looking approach.

Bibliography

Accominotti, Olivier, *London Merchant Banks, the Central Europe-an Panic, and the Sterling Crisis of 1931*, Cambridge University Press, 2012

Accominotti, Olivier, *International Monetary Regimes: The Interwar Gold Exchange Standard, in Handbook of the History of Money and Currency*, Springer Nature, Singapore, 2020.

Accominotti, Olivier and Eichengreen, Barry, *The Mother of all Sud-den Stops: Capital Flows and Reversals in Europe, 1919–32*, The Economic History Review, 2015.

Adams, J. *The Exchange-Rate Mechanism in the European Monetary System*, Bank of England Quarterly Bulletin 30, no. 4, 1990.

Alesina, Alberto with Acemoglu, Daron and Bickerton, Christo-pher J., *The Search for Europe: Contrasting Approaches*, BBVA, 2016.

Alesina, Alberto with Ardagna, Silvia and Galasso, Vincenzo, *The Euro and Structural Reforms*, NBER Working Paper No. 14479, 2008.

Arcelli Angelo Federico, *Considerations about the historical reasons behind the limits of current Eurozone architecture*. In: Gennaro A; Masera, R.; Velo D; Capriglione F; Preziosa P; Pelanda C; Chiarelli R; Carli F; Giovannini R, Arcelli A. (editors): Genn-aro A; Masera R, *Riflessioni sul futuro dell'Europa*. p. 157–164,

Roma: Aracne Editrice srl, ISBN: 978-88255-3728-4—April 2020.

Arcelli Angelo Federico, Fay Robert, Tria Giovanni, *The World with and after COVID19*, Center for International Governance Innovation (CIGI), December 2021.

Arcelli Angelo Federico, Gorino Chiara, Torcellan Claudio, *Le prospettive del credito in Italia dopo la crisi pandemica e l'attesa fine del Temporary Framework*—su "Rivista Bancaria"—Minerva Bancaria, vol. 4–5–6, p. 156–175, ISSN: 1594-7556, 2021.

Arcelli Angelo Federico, Gorino Chiara and Torcellan, Claudio, *La situazione del Mercato del credito in Italia dopo la pandemia e in vista della fine del 'Temporary Framework' europeo*, Quaderni DISES, no. 152/September 2022, Piacenza: Dipartimento di Scienze Economiche e Sociali, Università Cattolica del Sacro Cuore, available at: https://dipartimenti.unicatt.it/dises-Arcelli-Gorino-Torcellan_152.pdf.

Arcelli Angelo Federico and Marchetto, Agostino, *Communion - reflections for an intraecclesial dialogue*, Editore Rubbettino, October 2021.

Arcelli Angelo Federico and Marchetto, Agostino, *Dialogue. Open Reflections in a Phase of Transition*, Editore Rubbettino, ISBN 9788875744687, December 2023.

Arcelli Angelo Federico and Marchetto Agostino, *Riflessioni per un dialogo intraecclesiale* Editore Rubbettino—ISBN: 978-88-498-6802-9—June 2021.

Arcelli Angelo Federico, Masera Rainer Stefano, Tria Giovanni, *Da Versailles a Bretton Woods: errori storici e modelli ancora attuali per un sistema monetario internazionale sostenibile*, in Moneta e Credito, Rome, December 2021.

Arcelli Angelo Federico, Moavero Milanesi Enzo (editors), *Le prospettive dell'Unione europea: i profili chiave e i nodi da sciogliere.*

Editore Rubbettino, Atti della XVIII Lezione Mario Arcelli, October 2022.

Arcelli Angelo Federico, Padoan Pietro Carlo, *Data's Transformative Power: Opportunities, Risks and Privacy*, Center for International Governance Innovation (CIGI), December 2023.

Arcelli Angelo Federico, Padoan Pietro Carlo (editors), *NextGenEU: un motore di crescita per l'Europa?*, Editore Rubbettino, Atti della XIX Lezione Mario Arcelli, October 2023.

Arcelli Angelo Federico, Privitera Alexander, *IMF Special Drawing Rights allocation as a first step towards a new economic order*, ISEA Centro Studi, 2022.

Arcelli Angelo Federico, Torcellan Claudio, *Un nuovo e imprevedibile contesto.* "Rivista Bancaria"—Minerva Bancaria, vol. Gennaio—Aprile 2022, p. 141–147, ISSN: 1594-7556.

Arcelli Angelo Federico and Siniscalco Domenico (editors), *L'economia politica della pandemia.* Collection of articles by Siniscalco D., Cottarelli C., Masera R.S., Tria G., Arcelli A.F., Timpano F.—Editore Rubbettino, Atti della XVII Lezione Mario Arcelli, ISBN: 978-88-498-6833-3—July 2021.

Arcelli Angelo Federico and Tria Giovanni, *Time to reset?*—World Commerce Review, ISSN: 1751-0023—2021.

Arcelli Angelo Federico and Tria Giovanni, *The post pandemic economic order* in Longitude, p. 56–64, ISSN: 2039-554X. 2021.

Arcelli Angelo Federico and Tria Giovanni, *Towards a Renewed Bretton Woods Agreement*, Washington, DC, Transatlantic Leadership Network—ISBN: 978-0-9600127-8-7—January 2021.

Arcelli Angelo Federico, Tria Giovanni and Federico Andrea, *Blockchain Technology and Crypto assets as a New Form of Payment Tool.* Center for International Governance Innovation (CIGI), 2020.

Arslanalp, Serkan with Eichengreen, Barry and Simpson-Bell, Chima, *The stealth erosion of dollar dominance and the rise of nontraditional reserve currencies*, Journal of International Economics, Volume 138, https://doi.org/10.1016/j.jinteco.2022.103656 (https://www.sciencedirect.com/science/article/pii/S0022199622000885), 2022.

Bartel, Rogier J. *International Monetary Unions: the Nineteenth Century Experience*, The Journal of European Economic History, 1974.

Battistini, Niccolò with Pagano, Marco and Simonelli, Saverio, *Systemic Risk, Sovereign Yields and Bank Exposures in the Euro Crisis*, Economic Policy Vol. 29, Issue78, 2014.

Begg, David et al. *Monitoring European Integration: The Impact of Eastern Europe*, Centre for Economic and Policy Research, London, 1990.

Bech, Morten L. and Garratt, Rodney: "*Central Bank Cryptocurrencies*", BIS Quarterly Review, September 2017.

BIS "*Central banks and payments in the digital era*", Glossary to the Annual Economic Report, Chapter III, Basel, 2020.

Bergsten, Fred, *The Dollar and the Euro*, Foreign Affairs 76, 2004.

Bernanke, Ben Shlomo, *The World on a Cross of Gold: A Review of "Golden Fetters": The Gold Standard and the Great Depression, 1919–1939*, Journal of Monetary Economics, 1993.

Bernanke, Ben Shlomo with James, Harold, *The Gold Standard, Deflation, and Financial Crisis in the Great Depression: An International Comparison*, NBER Working Paper No. 3488, 1990.

Bernanke, Ben Shlomo with James, Harold, *The Gold Standard, Deflation, and Financial Crisis in the Great Depression: An International Comparison*, Chapter in Financial Markets and Financial Crises, University of Chicago Press, 1991.

Bernanke, Ben Shlomo with Laubach, Thomas; Mishkin, Frederic and Posen, Adam, *Inflation Targeting: Lessons from the International Experience*, Princeton University Press, Princeton, 1999.

Bernanke, Ben Shlomo with Mishkin, Frederic, *Central Bank Behavior and the Strategy of Monetary Policy: Observations from Six Industrialized Countries*, NBER Working Paper No. 4082, 1992.

Blakemore, Erin, *The Euro: How a Common Currency Helped Europe Achieve Peace*, History Stories, 2018.

Bloomfield, Arthur I. *Monetary Policy Under the International Gold Standard: 1880–1914*, Federal Reserve Bank of New York, New York, 1959.

Bolt, Jutta and van Zanden, Jan Luiten, *Maddison style estimates of the evolution of the world economy: A new 2023 update*, Journal of Economic Surveys, 1–41, 2024.

Boltho, Andrea with Carlin, Wendy, *The Problems of European Monetary Union—Asymmetric Shocks or Asymmetric Behavior*, VOXEU CEPR, 2012.

Bordo, Michael D. *A Brief History of Central Banks*, Federal Reserve Bank of Cleveland, Cleveland, 2007.

Bordo, Michael D., *The Bretton Woods International Monetary System: A Historical Overview*, in *A Retrospective on the Bretton Woods System: Lessons for International Monetary Reform* by Michael D. Bordo and Barry Eichengreen, University of Chicago Press, 1993.

Bordo, Michael D., *The Gold Standard, Bretton Woods and other Monetary Regimes: An Historical Appraisal*, NBER Working Paper No. 4310, 1993.

Bordo, Michael D., *The Operation and Demise of the Bretton Woods System; 1958 to 1971*, Chicago University Press, Chicago, 2017.

Bordo, Michael D. with Dittmar, Robert D. and Gavin, William T., *Gold, Fiat, and Price Stability*, NBER Working Paper No. 10171, 2003.

Bordo, Michael D. with Eichengreen, Barry, *The Rise and Fall of a Barbarous Relic: The Role of Gold in the International Monetary System*, Chicago University Press, Chicago, 1998.

Bordo, Michael D. with James, Harold, *The Great Depression Analogy*, NBER Working Paper No. 15584.

Bordo, Michael D. with Jonung, Lars, *The Future of the EMU: What Does the History of Monetary Union Tell Us?* NBER Working Paper No. 7365, 1999.

Bordo, Michael D. with MacDonald, Ronald, *The Inter-War Gold Exchange Standard: Credibility and Monetary Independence*, NBER Working Papers No. w8429, 2001.

Bordo, Michael D. with Murshid, Antu P., *The International Transmission of Financial Crises before World War II: Was there Contagion?* Rutgers University, 1999.

Bordo, Michael D. with Orphanides, Athanasios, *The Great Inflation: The Rebirth of Modern Central Banking*, Chicago University Press, Chicago, 2013.

Bordo, Michael D. with Schwartz, Anna J., *A Retrospective on the Classical Gold Standard, 1821–1931*, Chicago University Press, Chicago, 1984.

Bordo, Michael D. with Siklos, Pierre L., *Central Bank Credibility: An Historical and Quantitative Exploration, in Central Bank at a Crossroads*, Cambridge University Press, Cambridge, 2016.

Bordo, Michael D. with Pierre L. Siklos *Central Banks: Evolution and Innovation in Historical Perspective*, NBER Working Paper No. 23847, Cambridge.

Bordo, Michael D. with Simard Dominique and White, Eugene, *France and the Bretton Woods International Monetary System: 1960–1968*, Chicago University Press, Chicago, 1994.

Boughton, James M., *Why White, Not Keynes? Inventing the Postwar International Monetary System*, IMF Working Paper/02/52, 2002.

Branson, William, *German Unification and the Breakdown of the EMS, and the Transition to Stage III*, in David Cobham (ed.), European Monetary Upheavals, Manchester University Press, Manchester, 1994.

Bunker, Nick, *Declining U.S. Labor Mobility is About More than Geography*, Washington Center for Equitable Growth, 2016.

Buchanan, James, *John Law: A Scottish Adventurer of the Eighteenth Century*, MacLehose Press, 2018.

Calvo, Guillermo A. with Reinhart, Carmen M., *Fear of Floating*, The Quarterly Journal of Economics, Volume 117, Issue 2, 2002.

Capie, Forrest with Goodhart, Charles; Schnadt, Norbel, *The Development of Central Banking*, Cambridge University Press, Cambridge, UK, 2012.

Carbaugh, Robert L., *The Weakened Snake: Exchange Market Adjustments*, Nebraska Journal of Economics and Business, Vol. 16, No. 1, Creighton University, 1977.

Carney, Mark S. *The Growing Challenges for Monetary Policy in the Current International Monetary and Financial System*, Jackson Hole Symposium, 2019.

Cassel, Gustav, *The Downfall of the Gold Standard*, Oxford University Press, 1936.

Cesarano, Filippo, *Defining Fundamental Disequilibrium: Keynes's Unheeded Contribution*, Journal of Economic Studies, 2003.

Cesarano, Filippo, *Monetary Theory and Bretton Woods: The Construction of an International Monetary Order*, Cambridge University Press, Cambridge and New York, 2006.

Chinn, Menzie D., Ito, Hiro and McCauley, Robert N., *Do Central Banks Rebalance Their Currency Shares?* NBER Working Paper No. w29190 (August), 2021.

Chinn, Menzie D. with Frankel, Jeffrey A. and Ito, Hiro, *The dollar versus the euro as international reserve currencies, Journal of International Money and Finance*, https://doi.org/10.1016/j.jimonfin.2024.103123 (https://www.sciencedirect.com/science/article/pii/S0261560624001104), 2024.

Choudhri, Ehsan U. Kochin, Levis A., *The Exchange Rate and the International Transmission of Business Cycle Disturbances: Some Evidence from the Great Depression*, Journal of Money, Credit and Banking, 1980.

Christiano, Lawrence J. with Motto, Roberto and Rostag¬no, Massimo, *The Great Depression and the Friedman-Schwartz Hypothesis*, NBER Working Paper No. 10255, 2004.

Cimadomo, Jacopo with Hauptmeier, Sebastian, Palazzo, Alessandra Anna and Popov, Alexander, *Risk Sharing in the Euro Area*, ECB Economic Bulletin, Issue 3, 2018.

Coffey, Peter with Presley, John, *European Monetary Integration*, Macmillan Press, London, 1971.

Cohen, Benjamin with Subacchi, Paola, *A One-and-a-Half Currency System*, Journal of International Affairs 62(1), 2008.

Coeuré, Benoit, *Should the ECB Care About the Euro's Global Role?* Voxeu, 2019.

Cooper, Richard N., *The Gold Standard: Historical Facts and Future Prospects*, Brookings Papers on Economic Activity, 1982.

Crafts, Nicholas and Fearon, Peter, *Lessons from the 1930s Great Depression*, Oxford Review of Economic Policy, 2010.

Dabrowski, Marek, *The Economic and Monetary Union: Past, Present and Future*, Policy Department for Economic, Scientific and Quality of Life Policies, 2019.

Delivorias, Angelos, *A History of European Monetary Integration*, European Parliamentary Research Service, 2015.

De Grauwe, Paul with Verfaille, Guy, *Exchange Rate Variability, Misalignment and the European Monetary System*, University Chicago Press, Chicago, 1988.

De Kock, Michiel Hendrik, *On Central Banking*, St Martin's Press, New York, 1975.

Dincer, Nergiz and Eichengreen, Barry, *Central Bank Transparency and Independence: Updates and New Measures*, International Journal of Central Banking, 2014.

Edvinsson, Rodney with Jacobson, Tor and Waldenström, Daniel, *Sveriges Riksbank and the History of Central Banking*, Cambridge University Press, 2018.

Eichengreen, Barry, *Central Bank Cooperation Under the Interwar Gold Standard*, Explorations in Economic History, 1984.

Eichengreen, Barry, *The Bank of France and the Sterilization of Gold, 1926–1932*, Explorations in Economic History, 1986.

Eichengreen, Barry, *The Breakup of the Euro Area*, NBER Working Paper No. 13393, 2007.

Eichengreen, Barry, *The EMS Crisis in Retrospect*, NBER Working Paper No. 8035, 2000.

Eichengreen, Barry, *Exorbitant Privilege. The Rise and Fall of the Dollar and the Future of the International Monetary System*, Oxford University Press, Oxford, 2010.

Eichengreen, Barry, *Golden Fetters: The Gold Standard and the Great Depression, 1919–1939*, Oxford University Press, Oxford, 1992.

Eichengreen, Barry, *Sui Generis EMU*, NBER Working Paper No. 13740, 2008.

Eichengreen, Barry, *Three Perspectives on the Bretton Woods System*, NBER Working Paper No. 4141, 1992.

Eichengreen, Barry and Flandreu, Marc, *The Gold Standard in Theory and History*, Routledge, London, 1997.

Eichengreen, Barry and Sachs, Jeffrey, *Exchange Rates and Economic Recovery in the 1930s*, Cambridge University Press, 2009.

Einaudi Luca, *A Historical Perspective on the Euro: The Latin Monetary Union (1865–1926)*, ifo DICE Report, 2018.

Einaudi, Luca, *From the Franc to the 'Europe': Great Britain, Germany and the attempted transformation of the Latin Monetary Union into a European Monetary Union*, Economic History Review 53 (2), 284–308, 2000.

Einaudi, Luca, *Money and Politics: European Monetary Unification and the International Gold Standard (1865–1873)*, Oxford University Press, 2001.

Elwell, Craig K., *Brief History of the Gold Standard in the United States*, Congressional Research Service, 2001.

Endres, Anthony M., *Currency Competition: A Hayekian Perspective on International Monetary Integration*, 2009.

European Central Bank (2023–24). *The International Role of the Euro*: https://www.ecb.europa.eu/press/other-publications/ire/html/ecb.ire202406~0b56ba4f71.en.html https://www.ecb.europa.eu/press/other-publications/ire/html/ecb.ire202306~d334007ede.en.html

Farrell, Henry Newman, Abraham L., *Weaponized Interdependence. How Global Economic Networks Shape State Coercion*, International Security, Vol. 44, No. 1, 2019.

Feldstein, Martin, *The Political Economy of the European Economic and Monetary Union: Political Sources of an Economic Liability*, NBER Working Paper No. 6150, 1998.

Fendel, Ralph and Maurer, D., *Does European History Repeat Itself? Lessons from the Latin Monetary Union for the European Monetary Union*, Journal of Economic Integration, 2015.

Ferguson, Niall, *The Cash Nexus: Money and Power in the Modern World 1700–2000*, Basic Books, New York, 2001.

Filtri A. et al., *Digital Euro: The Ecb Saving Europe Again*, Mediobanca Securities, London, March 8th, 2021.

FED, Global Uncertainty Index, retrieved from stlouisfed. org, February 26th, 2022.

FED, *The international role of the Dollar* (June 2023): https://www.federalreserve.gov/econres/notes/feds-notes/the-international-role-of-the-us-dollar-post-covid-edition-20230623.html

Flandreu, Marc, *The Economics and Politics of Monetary Unions: a Reassessment of the Latin Monetary Union*, 1865–71, Financial Historic Review, 2000.

Flandreu, Marc, *On the Inflationary Bias of Common Currencies: The Latin Union Puzzle,* European Economic Review, North-Holland, 1993.

Flandreau, Marc, *Was the Latin Monetary Union a Franc Zone?* In: Reis J. (eds) International Monetary Systems in Historical Perspective, Palgrave Macmillan, London, 1995.

Fratianni, Michele and Spinelli, Franco, *A Monetary History of Italy*, Cambridge University Press, Cambridge, 1997.

Frankel, Jeffrey and Phillips, Steven, *The European Monetary System: Credible at Last?* NBER Working Paper No. 3819, 1991.

Frieden, Jeffry A., *Monetary Populism in Nineteenth Century America: An Open Economy Interpretation*, Journal of Economic History, 1997.

Froot, Kenneth A. with Rogoff, Kenneth, *The EMS, the EMU and the Transition to a Common Currency*, Chapter in NBER book NBER Macroeconomics Annual 1991, Vol. 6, 1991.

Garber, Peter M., *The Collapse of the Bretton Woods Fixed Exchange Rate System*, in A Retrospective on the Bretton Woods System: Lesson for International Monetary Reform, University of Chicago Press, 1993.

Giavazzi, Francesco with Pagano, Marco, *The Advantage of Tying One's Hands: EMS Discipline and Central Bank Credibility*, European Economic Review 32, 1998.

Gensler G., *Remarks before the Aspen Security Forum*, Sec, August 3rd, 2021.

Goldberg, Linda S., *Banking Globalization, Transmission, and Monetary Policy Autonomy*, Federal Reserve Bank of New York, 2013.

Goldberg, Linda S. and Hannaoui, Oliver, *Drivers of Dollar Share in Foreign Exchange Reserves*, Federal Reserve Bank of New York Staff Reports, no. 1087, March 2024, https://doi.org/10.59576/sr.1087, 2024.

Goodhart, Charles, *The Bank of England, 1694–2017*, Cambridge University Press, 2018.

Goodhart Charles, *Problems of Monetary Management: the UK Experience*, Papers in Monetary Economics, Reserve Bank of Australia, 1975.

Greenspan Alan, *Hearing, House Oversight Committee*, Us Congress, Proceedings, October 23rd, 2008.

Habermeier, Karl with Kokenyne, Annamaria Romaine and Anderson, Veyrune & Harald, *Revised System for the Classification of Exchange Rate Arrangements*, IMF Working Paper, 2009.

Hall, Peter A., *Varieties of Capitalism and the Euro Crisis*, West European Politics 37, 2014.

Hall, Peter A., *The Euro Crisis and the Future of European Integration*, BBVA, Madrid, 2016.

Hamilton, James D., *Role of the International Gold Standard in Propagating the Great Depression*, Contemporary Policy Issues, 1988.

Harold, James, *International Monetary Cooperation Since Bretton Woods*, International Monetary Fund, Washington DC, 1996.

Harold, James, *The End of Globalization: Lessons from the Great Depression*, Harvard University Press, 2002.

Hayek, Friedrich A., *Choice in Currency: A Way to Stop Inflation*, The Institute of Economic Affairs, 1976.

Hicks J., *Causality in Economics*, Blackwell, Oxford, 1979.

Hix, Simon, *What's Wrong with the European Union and How to Fix It*, Cambridge: Polity, 2008.

Höpner, Martin, *Better Than the Euro? The European Monetary System (1979–1998)*, 2017.

IPCC, *The Concept of Risk in the Sixth Assessment Report*, Geneva, September 4th, 2020.

Ikenberry, John G., *A World Economy Restored: Expert Consensus and the Anglo-American Power Settlement*, The MIT Press, 1990.

Ikenberry, John G., *The Political Origins of Bretton Woods*, in A Retrospective on the Bretton Woods System: Lesson for International Monetary Reform, University of Chicago Press, 1993.

Ilzetzki, Ethan with Reinhart, Carmen M. and Rogoff, Kenneth S., *Why is the Euro Punching Below its Weight?* NBER Working Paper No. 26760, 2020.

International Monetary Fund, *The Snake in the Tunnel: Eventual monetary union in the EEC may involve reducing exchange rate fluctuations among the currencies of the nine member countries,*, by Günter Wittich and Masaki Shiratori, June 1st, 1973: https://www.elibrary.imf.org/view/journals/022/0010/002/article-A002-en.xml

International Monetary Fund. *World Uncertainty Index, Sixty Years of Uncertainty*, in Finance and Development, March 2020.

Irwin, Douglas A., *The Missing Bretton Woods Debate Over Flexible Exchange Rates*, NBER Working Paper No. 23037, 2017.

Ito, Hiro, and McCauley, Robert, "*Currency Composition of Foreign Exchange Reserves*". Journal of International Money and Finance, Volume 102 (April 2020; 102–104), 2020.

Kee-Hong Bae and Bailey, Warren, *The Latin Monetary Union: Some evidence on Europe's failed common currency*, Review of Development Finance, p. 131–149, 2011.

Keynes, John Maynard, *Proposals for an International Clearing Union, in Keith Horsefield et al, The International Monetary Fund 1945–1965: Twenty Years of International Monetary Cooperation*, Volume 1. Chronicle, International Monetary Fund, Washington DC, 1943.

Keynes, John Maynard, *The Collected Writings*. Vol. 26, Activities, 1941–46: Shaping the Post-War World: Bretton Woods and Reparations, London: Macmillan, 1980.

Kindleberger, Charles P., *Manias, Panics and Crashes*, Wiley Investment Classics, 1996.

Kindleberger, Charles P., *A Financial History of Western Europe*, Oxford University Press, 1993.

Krugman, Paul R. with Obstfeld, Maurice; Melitz, Marc J., *International Economics, Theory and Policy*, Pearson, United Kingdom, Chapter 19, pp. 598–609, 2018

Kugler, Peter, *The Bretton Woods System: Design and Operation, in Money in the Western Legal Tradition*, Oxford University Press, Oxford, 2016.

Mackay, Charles, *The Mississippi Scheme*, Andrew Publishing Company, London, Reprint of the 1885 Edition, 1980.

Masera Rainer, *Leverage and Risk-Weighted Capital in Banking Regulation*, in The Journal of Bank Management, February 2020.

Masera Rainer, *Old and New Risks: Challenges Ahead*, Enel Risk Academy, Rome, November 9th, 2021.

Massad, Carlos *Regulating Stable Currencies Isn't Just About Avoiding Systemic Risk*, Brookings, October 5th, 2020.

Matthijs, Matthias with Blyth, Mark, *The Future of the Euro*, Oxford University Press, 2015.

McKinnon, Ronald I., *The Rules of the Game: International Money in Historical Perspective*, Journal of Economic Literature, 1993.

McKinnon, Ronald I., *The Unloved Dollar Standard: From Bretton Woods to the Rise of China*, Oxford University Press, New Yor, 2014k.

Meissner, Christopher M., *A New World Order: Explaining the Emergence of the Classical Gold Standard*, NBER Working Paper No. 9233, 2002.

Meltzer, Allan H., *U.S. Policy in the Bretton Woods Era*, Federal Reserve Bank of St. Louis Review 73, 1991.

Mitchener, Kris James with Wandschneider, Kirsten, *Capital Controls and Recovery from the Financial Crisis of the 1930s*, Journal of International Economics 95, 2015.

Mitchener, Kris J. with Masato Shizume and Weidenmier, Marc D., *Why Did Countries Adopt the Gold Standard? Lessons from Japan*, NBER Working Paper No. 15195, 2009.

Moggridge, D. E., *British Monetary Policy 1924–1931: The Norman Conquest of $4.86*, Cambridge University Press, Cambridge, 1972.

Mooslechner, Peter and Gnan, Enest, *The Experience of Exchange Rate Regimes in Southeastern Europe in a Historical and Comparative Perspective*, Proceedings of OeNB Workshops, Vienna, 2007.

Moure, Kenneth, *The Gold Standard Illusion: France, the Bank of France, and the International Gold Standard, 1914–1939*, Oxford University Press, 2002.

Obstfeld, Maurice, *The adjustment mechanism, chapter in A Retrospective on the Bretton Woods System: Lessons for International Monetary Reform*, University of Chicago Press, 1993.

Obstfeld, Maurice with Rogoff, Kenneth, *The Mirage of Fixed Exchange Rates*, Journal of Economic Perspectives, 1995.

Ohanian, Lee E., *What—or Who—Started the Great Depression?* NBER Working Paper No. 15258, 2009.

Oliver Wyman Forum, AWS: *"Retail Central Bank, Digital Currency: From Vision to Design—A framework to align policy objectives and technology design choices"*, March 2022.

Panetta Fabio, *Presente e futuro della moneta nell'era digitale*, Lectio Cooperativa, Federcasse, Roma, December 10th, 2020.

Parker Willis, H., *A History of The Latin Monetary Union: A Study of International Monetary Action*, The University of Chicago Press, Chicago, 1901.

Pollard, Patricia S., *The Creation of the Euro and the Role of the Dollar in International Markets*, The Federal Reserve Bank of St. Louis, 2001.

Pollard, Sydney, *The Integration of the European Economy since 1815,* Economic History, 1981.

Prasad Eswar, *China's Digital Yuan,* in Fortune, February 1st, 2022.

Redish, Angela, *The Latin Monetary Union and the emergence of the international gold standard.* In M. Bordo & F. Capie, Monetary Regimes in Transition (Studies in Macroeconomic History), Cambridge University Press, Cambridge, 1993.

Reuven Glick and Rose, Andrew K., *Currency Unions and Trade: A Post-EMU Mea Culpa,* NBER Working Paper No. 21535, 2015.

Rogoff, Kenneth A., *The Optimal Degree of Commitment to an Intermediate Monetary Target,* Quarterly Journal of Economics 100, 1985.

Rueff, Jacques, *The Monetary Sin of the West,* pag. 78, The Macmillan Company, 866 Third Avenue, New York, N.Y. 10022 Collier-Macmillan Canada Ltd., Toronto, Ontario—The Monetary Sin of the West was originally published in French by Librairie Plon under the title *Le Péché Monêtàire de l'Occident* and is reprinted by permission. Library of Congress Catalog Card Number: 79-182450, Second Printing, 1972.

Savona, Paolo, *Features of an Economics with Cryptocurrencies,* Lectio Magistralis, Università di Cagliari, October 1st, 2021.

Schenk, Catherine, *The Decline of Sterling: Managing the Retreat of an International Currency, 1945 to 1992,* Cambridge University Press, New York, 2010.

Schwartz, Anna J., *Alternative Monetary Regimes: The Gold Standard,* in Money in Historical Perspective, University of Chicago Press, 1987.

Schwartz, Anna J., *Lessons of the Gold Standard Era and the Bretton Woods System for the Prospects of an International Monetary System Constitution,* in Money in Historical Perspective, University of Chicago Press, 1987.

Selgin, George, *The Rise and Fall of the Gold Standard in the United States*, Cato Institute, Policy Analysis No. 729, 2013.

Shambaugh, Jay C., *The Euro's Three Crises*, Brookings Papers on Economic Activity, The Brookings Institution, 2012.

Solomon, Robert, *The International Monetary System, 1945–1976; An Insider's View*, Harper and Row, New York, 1976.

Solomon, Robert, *The International Monetary System, 1945–1981*, Harper & Row, 1982.

Steil, Benn, *The Battle of Bretton Woods: John Maynard Keynes, Harry Dexter White, and the Making of a New World Order*, Princeton University Press, Princeton, 2014.

Stiglitz, Joseph E., *The Euro: How a Common Currency Threatens the Future of Europe*, W. W. Norton & Company, New York, 2016.

Syrrakos, Dimitrios, *A Reassessment of the Werner Plan and the Delors Report: Why did they Experience a Different Fate?* Comparative Economic Studies 52, 2010.

Takekazu, Iwamoto, *The Keynes Plan for an International Clearing Union*, The Kyoto University Economic Review, 1997.

Temin, Peter, *The Great Depression*, NBER Historical Working Paper No. 62, 1994.

Thedéen Erik, Risinger B., *"Crypto-Assets Are a Threat to the Climate Transition"*, Swedish Financial Authority, Stockholm, November 5th, 2021.

Tria Giovanni, Arcelli Angelo Federico, *Towards a Renewed Bretton Woods Agreement*, Washington, DC, Transatlantic Leadership Network—ISBN: 978-0-9600127-8-7—January 2021.

Triffin, Robert, *Gold and the Dollar Crisis*, New Haven: Yale University Press, 1960.

Vanthoor, W. F. V., *European Monetary Union Since 1848: a Political and Historical Analysis*, Cheltenham, 1996.

Verdun Amy with Jones, Erik, *The Werner Report of 1970—a blueprint for EMU in the EU?* EUSA, Miami, 2017.

Wandschneider, Kirsten, *The Stability of the Interwar Gold Exchange Standard: Did Politics Matter?* The Journal of Economic History, 2008.

Weizhen, Tan, *The Growing US Deficit Raises Questions About Funding as China Cuts U.S. Debt Holdings*, CNBC, 2020.

Werner Committee, *Report to the council and the commission on the realization by stages of economic and monetary union in the community (Werner Report)*, Bulletin of European Communities, Supplement 11, 1970.

Wheelock, David C., *Monetary Policy in the Great Depression and Beyond: The Sources of the Fed's Inflation Bias*, Federal Reserve Bank of St. Louis, 1997.

Wolf, Nikolaus, *Scylla and Charybdis. Explaining Europe's Exit from Gold, January 1928-December 1936*, CESifo Working Paper Series 2271, 2008.

Zhou Xiaochuan, *Reform the International Monetary System*, Bank for International Settlements, Basel, Switzerland, 2009.